5000 Years of Foreplay

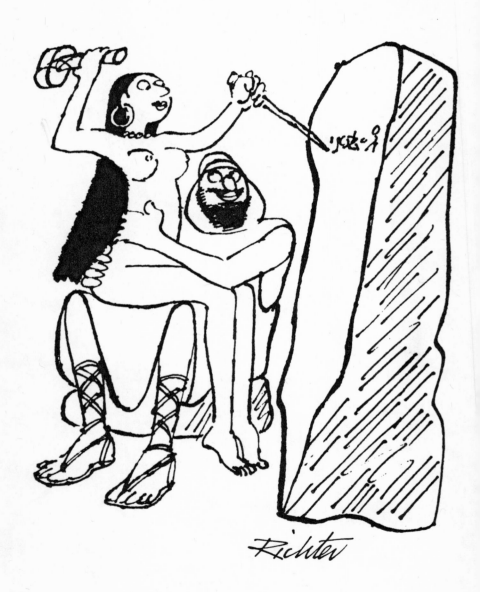

5000 YEARS
of
FOREPLAY

by Ira Wallach

Illustrations by Mischa Richter

William Morrow and Company, Inc.
New York   1976

Library of Congress Cataloging in Publication Data

Wallach, Ira Jan (date)
  5000 years of foreplay.

  1. Sex—Anecdotes, facetiae, satire, etc.
I. Title.
HQ454.W34   301.41′7′0207   75-22308
ISBN 0-688-02966-3

Book design by H. Roberts

Contents

5000 Years of Foreplay

I
Yussuf ibn Farad,
Essene Swinger

This year the warm-blooded world, with the possible exception of the Reverend Norman Vincent Peale, celebrates the five thousandth anniversary of a seminal event: the discovery of foreplay.

According to authorities such as Hitchcock, Babcock, and Cockburn, Neanderthal man, stumbling blindly through Europe during the Würm glacial period, took the first barbaric steps toward the creation of foreplay by indulging in a primeval form of sexual activity known as "messing around." Adcock and Cockcroft, however, dispute this theory, claiming that Neanderthal man did not reach even that level of sexual sophistication, but the weight of the evidence lies with Leacock, Peacock, and Hancock.

Almost all recognized sex historians agree that in the Western Hemisphere during the Aftonian interglacial epoch, the inhabitants of North America had already discovered deep petting, but they used this technique in so random and casual a fashion that we cannot yet classify it as a true form of foreplay. And according to Penix, whose monumental study of the Aleut orgasm remains a classic, hanky-panky was widespread during the Paleolithic era.

Scientists have generally accepted 3025 B.C. as the year that Yussuf ibn Farad, a highly hormonal Essene, first put foreplay into practice, and then popularized it until it became a societal fact of life throughout the world.

Yussuf's accomplishment has come down to us in the form of legend, but as in so many other legends, fancy cloaks the solid bones of truth. The legend has it that Yussuf came upon a Shulamite shepherdess with paisley ears who wore a flowing see-through djellaba. Yussuf at once made a suggestion, to which she responded by firmly crossing her legs. It appears that the Shulamite had sworn a three-hour vow of chastity, and the vow had thirty-two minutes to go before expiration.

What to do with the thirty-two minutes? The imaginative Yussuf lay down beside the maiden, extended his hand, and began to stroke her left breast. She expressed sharp disapproval of this bizarre act, but since she was anointing his penis with frankincense and a pinch of myrrh as she spoke, Yussuf ignored her protestations. One thing led to another, and before the thirty-two minutes had passed, the tocsin rang out and foreplay was born!

After the vow expired Yussuf carried out what the Essenes would have called his original "game plan" or "scenario." Chronological hindsight suggests that the Shulamite's subsequent ecstasies were quite rococo.

Shortly thereafter Yussuf established the First Essene School of Ascetic Foreplay somewhere in the lascivious delta of the Tigris and the Euphrates.

It is ironic that the Grand Wizard of the Essenes later tried unsuccessfully to expel Yussuf from the order on a charge of rape—the very act he had refused to commit upon his buttery Shulamite. The council acquitted Yussuf, but he had to turn in his thorns. Thus with all pioneers!

This book is our attempt to sum up the sexual advances the human race has made since Yussuf ibn Farad. We hope in these pages to reach men and women all over the world who are anxious to grope their way toward a fuller, more time-consuming sex life, and more serial orgasms. Developments of recent years have finally given us reason to hope that we can achieve the goal toward which mankind has strained since the Garden of Eden—Permanent Orgasm. We are standing on the threshold of that apocalyptic breakthrough. Doubters will doubt, trashy people will enter demurrers, questioners will ask, "And who will do the laundry?" but no priggish King Canute can stop the tide of Permanent Orgasm.

We cannot conclude these opening remarks without expressing our thanks to many colleagues and friends who contributed so generously and selflessly with their carping criticism. We wish especially to express our debt to "H," the sensuous gila monster.

II

Sexual Positions
And How to Get Out of Them Without Injury

No matter how hotly we may deny it, we humans are proud animals, jealous of the positions we attain in life. This being so, why do we show only a desultory interest in assuming important positions when we engage ourselves in the very act which, if we are unlucky, produces life itself?

After an intense session of manual and labial foreplay, and a few careless raptures with an ostrich feather, the woman usually stretches out on her back, bends her legs at the knees, opens her thighs, and invites her lover to mount her face to face. That, of course, is the easy way in, and we call it the Missionary Position. Now it is not our intent to fling mud at a position that time and tradition have sanctified. Many great men, from Attila the Hun to Pëtr Ilich Tchaikovsky, were conceived in such a manner. Only nit-pickers or those to whom the bizarre is more important than creature comfort would deny that the Missionary Position has much to recommend it. It is comfortable. It is convenient. It meets the safety standards of all United States underwriters. And it is less likely than other positions to invite arch comments from friends.

But is it enough to be safe and comfortable? These

very words suggest denial of that Paphian ecstasy which all lovers seek. You cannot enrich your sex life if you are not bold and impetuous in exploring more dynamic sexual positions, positions that make you extend yourself in all directions and thereby force you to perform at higher levels of orgasmic delight. If some positions seem too labyrinthine, remember that the light at the end of the tunnel is an interstellar orgasm.

The timidity with which otherwise sophisticated people approach this subject is truly amazing. One would expect that "M," the erudite sexologist and author of that masterful work *The Sensuous Man,* would reflect none of this timidity. Yet in his book he speaks of such erotic ploys as *The Velvet Buzz Saw, The Runaway Pinch, The Butterfly Flick,* and *The Easy Rider* as though they were arcane rituals that only the inner circles of sexuality practice. Come now, "M"! Surely you must know these to be commonplace techniques that have even filtered down to blue-collar workers.

But where, on any page of *The Sensuous Man,* is one to find reference to *The Caterpillar Crawl, The Caribbean Cruise, The Persian Love Apple,* and the increasingly popular *McSorley's Flannel Tongue-Lash?* And therein lies the flaw in an otherwise profound book.

We can forgive "M" for omitting *Soixante-Neuf,* a maneuver so commonplace as to be vulgar, but how explain his failure to pay tribute to *The Cartwheel, Upsy-Daisy, Mabel-on-the-Table, Beat the Clock, Miss Muffet's Tuffet, Egg-in-the-Basket, Humpty-Dumpty, Apple Brown Betty, Frank-on-a-Roll,* and most particularly *Willy's Wheelbarrow?*

Let us begin our discussion of sexual positions with *The Cortney,* named for Hiram Cortney of Manchester, New Hampshire, who first developed the technique during Lent, 1954. *The Cortney* is designed for men and women

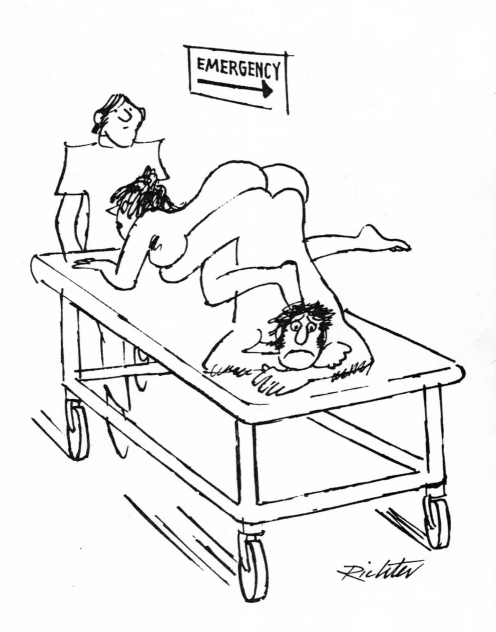

who like to make love on a library ladder. In this position the woman is ascendant. She places herself one rung above the man on the ladder. Her left foot should rest on a rung that bisects the man's lower leg between ankle and knee. She must then place her right foot two rungs higher, thus opening the inner thighs and making the vaginal area easily accessible.

The man, who has placed himself two rungs below her left foot, then goes into what is known as *The Cortney Shift*. Firmly grasping the woman's left buttock, he swings his right leg around until his right ankle is resting on the woman's right shoulder. Then, as the woman hangs on to the ladder for dear life, the man encircles her abdomen with his right hand. Thus positioned, he is now ready for entry, which must take place from the rear (*crevissade*) and at an angle of approximately 95° of upward thrust.

Do not be disappointed if you find entry difficult the first time. You and your loved one will work out the problems. You might even find it necessary to call in a third party to help you. If you are in a private library the housekeeper will lend a hand. If you are in a public library do not hesitate to call upon the services of the librarian. Her training has equipped her to assist the penetrating reader.

Do not let initial difficulties dampen your enthusiasm for *The Cortney*. With practice it will come easily to you, and you will regard it with the affection it truly deserves. *The Cortney* is best done in the reference section.

Tall in the Saddle is the position of choice for vertical, or standing, intercourse. Lovers use *Tall in the Saddle* for a quickie, or in circumstances where they find little room to lie down or even kneel. It is the position that Yussuf ibn Farad assumed whenever a large number of Essenes met in a small cave. *Crevissade,* or entry from the rear, is difficult when attempting a smart *Tall in the Saddle,* and lovers will do better to use the frontal entrance (*entressage de devant*). After achieving his *entressage,* the male partner should keep his hands in his pockets to avoid attracting undue attention.

Tall in the Saddle is a difficult position when the woman is considerably shorter than her lover. Therefore, in choosing a partner for *Tall in the Saddle* men should make height the first consideration. Do not let charm or appeal distract you. Stay away from shrimps, unless you consider the navel a good second best. If you can accomplish it, *Tall in the Saddle* makes a nice change of pace from *chaissage,* that manner of intercourse in a chair in which the woman sits backward with her nipples trapped in the lacework of the antimacassar.

Often at night a man may awake and discover that his bed partner is sleeping with her back to him and her legs slightly parted, in the position of an open scissors. Under these circumstances it is a simple matter for a man to make his penetration without waking the woman. This is known to lovers as *Scheherazade's Surprise.* We do not recommend *Scheherazade's Surprise* to men whose women are light sleepers.

Now we come to *The Hammer and Anvil.* We learned of this position from Fred Garner of Harvard, who was awarded a doctorate in foreplay by the 1964 Radcliffe graduating class. To prepare for *The Hammer and Anvil,* push a tall bureau or highboy to within three feet of the bed. You will also need a pulley affixed to the ceiling and capable of sustaining the woman's weight plus ten pounds (a safety factor). Sit the woman on top of the bureau or highboy. Run a length of rope under the woman's armpits and around the top of her chest, taking care to leave the breasts free, then draw the rope through the pulley. Let the loose ends of the rope fall to the bed where the man can manipulate them. The man then lies with his feet

dangling over the edge of the bed, and two plump pillows under his nates. Ask the woman on the bureau or highboy to sit with knees spread wide and arms akimbo to add a touch of insouciance. From the prone position the man must firmly grasp the pulley ropes and pull hard, thus raising the woman until she is suspended a few feet beneath the ceiling. Then, by exerting pressure on the ropes, he must make her sway back and forth as though she were on a child's swing. During this phase of *The Hammer and Anvil* the man must murmur endearments, to which she should respond in kind as she swings from the ceiling.

Timing is all-important in the next step. The man must carefully evaluate many factors: the pitch of sexual frenzy, the efficacy of the murmured endearments, and above all, the dimensions of the arc through which the woman is now swinging. A knowledge of the law of the pendulum will serve you well in this situation. Using split-second judgment, and without any warning to his companion, because the element of surprise is vital, the man must let go of the rope. Naturally, the woman will fall from the ceiling, but if he has timed every movement exactly right, she will impale herself on his penis in the astride, or *chevalade,* position, to the great joy of all concerned.

When first attempting *The Hammer and Anvil,* you must be prepared for a few failures. In this particular position women will often cry out, "You can't do this to me!" This is their way of saying, "Please don't stop!" Such are the mysteries of the language of love.

The Government Printing Office will shortly publish its *Handbook of Sexual Positions.* Although this is a political document designed to help Democrats deal with Republicans, it is a valuable compendium. Study this little volume wherever you may be. Take a copy to your shop or office. Form discussion groups where others can contribute to your knowledge of the niceties of the handbook. Limitations of space make it impossible for us to cover the subject as exhaustively as does this little treasure trove, but we would like to include two more positions which the Government somehow overlooked.

The first of these, *Neptune's Ledge,* is a dual-role position, meaning that the man and woman change places after the ninth orgasm. *Neptune's Ledge* requires a bathtub half-filled with warm strawberry yogurt. The woman must recline not in but on the rim of the tub. Her right leg should swing out so that her right foot is firmly placed on the bathroom floor. She must bend her left leg and keep her left foot on the tub rim. Then she folds her arms under her head. Under no conditions may she touch the yogurt, or she will be disqualified.

The man now stands on the bathroom floor and positions himself on a line with her navel. He puts his right leg into the tub of yogurt but keeps his left leg outside the tub. He then leans over and effects a frontal entry (*fleurissage,* or *entressage de devant*) while supporting himself with one hand on the edge of the tub and the other in the yogurt.

The danger of slipping in the yogurt adds a certain *frisson* to the excitement of this position. If you do slip, remember that most home-accident insurance policies cover you.

As we mentioned above, after the ninth orgasm the partners change positions and the woman has her turn to gambol in the yogurt.

The second position that the Government omitted from the handbook is called *Atlas Triumphant.* It is simplicity itself. The man and the woman stand close together on the floor, face to face. The woman then does a handstand. While on her hands, she twines her feet around the man's neck. The man then reaches down, seizes her wrists, and lifts her up until her face is on a level with his. With her legs around his neck, the woman is now open and ready for reception. The man then penetrates with ease. Once he has completed penetration, he jogs in place. The motion of the jogging will be enough to bring them both to climax.

It is important for the man to remember that he must maintain a firm grip on his partner's wrists throughout *Atlas Triumphant,* otherwise he risks the danger that she will drop to the floor with a dull thud. If, despite all precautions, you happen to drop your love partner, be tender as you minister to her bruises. A woman likes to feel wanted even though dropped.

Be adventurous. Devise your own positions. Who knows? Perhaps you may develop an All-American. If you do you can patent it and you will get a royalty every time it is used. (All-Americans will be awarded at the next session of the International Sex Conference, which will be held in Adelaide, Australia, over Sydney's objections.)

A word to our female readers. Remember that the proper use of the vaginal muscles will increase your pleasure and that of your partner no matter what position you use. Later in this book we will offer a series of suggested vaginal exercises that will enable you to perform many erotic miracles, such as smiling or frowning with your labia. (Cf. "Sexercises.") We have learned of one woman who can assume the astride (*chevalade*) position, remain perfectly still, and do needlepoint while bringing herself and her lover to climax solely by use of her vaginal muscles. Her needlepoint is excellent.

III

Sex Kits
For Sex Kittens and Tabbies

We know of one man who cannot perform the sex act satisfactorily unless he wears a stovepipe hat. Since he never knows whom he may meet in the course of his day, he wears it every place he goes. Some politicians now consider him a possible presidential candidate.

Do you find this odd? If so, you are blinding your mind and your heart to the glorious gadgetry that adds so much zest to free and unashamed sexual relations. It is absurd to content yourself with only those minimal gadgets that come with the human body. Would you buy an automobile without ordering a single one of those accessories the modern motorist finds indispensable?

Fortunately, in today's relaxed atmosphere millions of eager lovers recognize that they can and should use familiar objects around them to heighten the general excitement that leads to atomic-fission type orgasm. Follow this general rule: *if it looks as though it might fit, try it.*

Most of us are by now familiar with the usual hardware and rubber goods that lead us gently to our excruciating climax. The dildo is now as much at home in the bedroom as the eggbeater is in the kitchen. (Watch out for eggbeaters! They can lacerate mucous tissue.) Some women, in fact, would feel underdressed if they went out in public without wearing at least one dildo. Dildo-wearing is becoming a trend, and with good reason. Ask any woman who wears a dildo when she goes to the supermarket and she will tell you how it changes shopping from a chore into a glorious adventure.

Cordless vibrators are another popular source of feminine pleasure. Today women may go to almost any drugstore and purchase a vibrator shaped like their favorite penis. Since these vibrators ostensibly serve the purpose of general massage, the salesman will impute to you no ithyphallic motives. If he is a low-grade moron who emigrated from Albania four days ago and has not yet mastered English, he will have no idea to what purpose you intend to use the vibrator, so put aside any feeling of shame or embarrassment.

For lovers and other couples who like to practice economy, the electric toothbrush already in the bathroom makes an adequate stand-in for the vibrator. Use soft bristles or cover the head of the toothbrush with chamois soaked in sweet cream. (Again, if economy is important, half-and-half makes an acceptable substitute.)

Serious women who are not cavalier in their attitude toward orgasms now include in their sex kits broom handles, coke bottles (or diet-drink bottles for the obese), bud vases (careful, now!), and firm green bananas.

Men and women enjoy other items that are unisex in character. In this category we find the vacuum-cleaner hose, the garden hose for suburbanites and rustic bumpkins, Yorkshire pudding, and household pets.

Many men opt for the artificial vaginas, which come neatly folded in a plastic envelope. Once these vaginas were more or less uniform and designers based their models on a mythical "average." Today they come in a variety of sizes and styles, ranging from the baroque and rococo to the sternly modern. Many movie stars now model for vaginas as part of the promotion for their motion pictures. Since the worldwide success of the Italian film *Lost in a Dream,* millions of men keep a Mara Lucarelli vagina in the bureau drawer. Only the vagina of the English actress Laura Scott approaches the Lucarelli vagina in popularity.

Before ravishing an artificial vagina, pump it up with a warm nourishing soup until it is the right size to give your unique penis the pleasure it deserves. A word of advice. For reasons that modern psychiatry has not discovered, some intemperate women take umbrage when their lovers utilize an artificial vagina. In the words of one such woman, "I feel like a fifth wheel."

The element of sharing is important in the purchase of an artificial vagina. Therefore the wise man will consult his woman before adding this slyly amusing gewgaw to his sex kit. After all, it is only fair to ask for her color preferences. It would clearly be in poor taste if you bought such a vagina in a color that clashes with the general decor of the bedroom, particularly the sheets. Some ingenious men have solved this problem by ordering slipcovers for their artificial vaginas.

If you are a male, you might include a collection of corsets in your sex kit. You can study up on the subject by subscribing to *Corsets International,* a quarterly for connoisseurs. Become friendly with the proprietor of your neighborhood corset shop so that you can drop in at any time and feel the merchandise. The proprietor will enjoy chatting with you about stretchability and kindred subjects.

So far we have dealt only with the obvious items that we expect to find in even the most primitive of sex kits. Yet the imagination is a wonderful thing, and nothing, thank God, can inhibit the intellectual curiosity of the

monomaniacal lover. What we record here might not be everyone's cup of tea, but it may inspire you to explore further and stockpile your own arsenal of love.

One woman we know ordered a chic custom-made mink coat that buttons in the back for her dildo, and she has a hat to match. She and her husband are skilled in erotic experimentation and it was only recently that they came upon an implement that drives both of them wild: the kitchen mop. Now, just before intercourse and after considerable love play, he mops her down from head to foot. She claims that being mopped involves her entire body and inflames all her senses. For his part, the husband knows that he can always enjoy a clean love partner.

Another man has found pleasure in a curious reversal. In his sex kit he keeps a complete wardrobe for his wife. After he and she are nude they like to spend about thirty minutes in foreplay, dividing it up into sections. Ten minutes for tongue work, of which they set aside four for fellatio and six for cunnilingus; ten minutes for vibrator work; and five minutes for dildo work (two minutes anally, three minutes vaginally). Then the man takes his wife's wardrobe from the sex kit. He watches her slip into her panties, pull up her stockings, lean over and wriggle into her brassiere, draw on her shoes, step into her dress, zip it up, put on her scarf, and don her overcoat. As she puts her arms into the sleeves of the overcoat, he reaches orgasm and she opens a window because it is very hot in the room.

He is also one of the many who realize that no man's sex kit is complete without a penis ring adorned with either a sweetheart diamond or cactus spikes.

Perhaps this is the moment to issue a word of caution. Beware of developing too close a relationship with a foreign object. Sometimes addiction to these objects can affect the mutuality of a relationship. We know of one woman who left her husband to take up with a feather duster, and another who lost the affections of her lover to a pine knothole.

Edibles are classics that belong in every home sex kit. Whipped cream, of course, should always be available, because it is an all-purpose garnish that in true unisex fashion may be eaten from any part of the male or female body. It is also good on cake. Gourmet lovers make their own whipped cream. Others are content with the spray-can product, although we do not recommend it. Some find that spraying the beloved is a more emotional event than applying the whipped cream with the fingers or a spoon, but we believe this reaction to be most common among the emotionally immature. If you must use a spray can, shop for your whipped cream together until you find a brand that pleases you both.

Your acculturation will play a part in your choice of edibles. Jewish and Slavic lovers, for instance, often prefer sour cream to whipped cream, and Latins show a decided preference for guava paste. When using edibles in sex play, be sure to keep the windows closed to guard against flies.

A common weakness in men—or shall we call it a strength?—is the desire to dress their women in black, particularly black nighties, black panties, and black brassieres. One man bought his beloved a pair of Dr. Denton's, dyed them black, cut off the legs, and constructed portholes through which his lady's breasts could get a breath of fresh air. The very sight of his beloved in her Dr. Denton's is enough to bring him to instant erection.

Masks are always a happy addition to the sex kit. In the heat and furor of copulation it is a marvelous experience for a woman to look into the eyes of Joe Palooka or a prurient ape. And where is the man who can resist a woman wearing the mask of his mother?

Literally millions of knowledgeable men and women

-27

find rubber in any form a highly stimulating sexual come-on. Many a man will have his lady dress in nothing less than rubber panties, rubber hose, and rubber bra. Today, at almost any social gathering, we will see a number of women in modish rubber apparel and their presence will cause comment only among the uninitiated. These women, a bouncy lot, tend to band together and discuss the virtues of real rubber versus the new synthetics that some find so fulfilling. This rubber phenomenon is interesting because it illustrates the relationship between technology and sexual gratification. One would think that the passion for rubber had a centuries-old history, yet it was not until the end of the nineteenth century that rubber became available to us in quantity.

Unwittingly, cold technology continues to contribute to the warmth of love. Already common interest is drawing together circles of men whose greatest desire is to dress their women in bauxite. The allure of bauxite remains a mystery, but no one can deny the breath-catching effect of watching a woman slip out of a pair of bauxite panties and a bra. This year, at the opening of the Metropolitan Opera in New York City, many prominent socialites wore gowns of trailing bauxite that concealed bauxite panties with a trap door.

Fear, however, is invading the bauxite community. Tragically, we have no domestic source of bauxite. We are at the mercy of the foreign bauxite consortium, which is conspiring to quadruple the price of that lascivious metal. Perhaps it would be best to consult your pocketbook before succumbing to the bauxite lure.

What can we say that others have not said about the subtle vaginal fragrances tucked away in the modern woman's sex kit? Chocolate! Strawberry! Vanilla! Corned beef! Freesia! Gardenia! Pineapple soufflé! Fleur-de-lis! What infinite variety! Something to stimuate every taste bud! The value of these fragrances is obvious, and because of them many a man has turned to his beloved for satisfaction instead of running down to the corner for a beer or an ice-cream soda.

Have you applied crushed ice to your genitals lately? Crushed ice can greatly enhance the intensity of your orgasm. Keep an ice bucket next to your bed and try it tonight. Your genitals will love you for it. When rubbing crushed ice on the penis and the labia, remember that it melts rapidly. Lie on a rubber mat and keep a mop handy. You may use the same mop with which you plan to mop your sex partner. And when next you go to your neighborhood market, pick up a bag of pornographic ice cubes from the freezer.

Look around wherever you go and discover for yourself what new goodies you might add to your sex kit. Never go shopping without keeping love in mind. What amenable product does the A & P offer, Sears, Roebuck, the auto-parts store, the hardware department? Involve the entire gross national product in your lovemaking. You might even blaze new trails to that good old orgasm by doing something sexy with your discarded WIN button.

IV
Sexercises

A man need not be an Atlas nor a woman an Amazon to possess the stamina, proficiency, and skill to perform the act of love. Certainly good muscle tone, general health, and a fine set of teeth contribute greatly, but the average person is in good enough physical shape to expend the energy that run-of-the-mill lovemaking demands. Yet if you wish to bring subtlety to the lubricious bed, if you yearn to add abstruse and apocalyptic nuances to your *Frank-on-a-Roll,* if, in other words, you want to be not just a journeyman lover but a Heifetz of genital conjunction, then you must train to this end just as a prizefighter or a football player trains his or her body.

That is the purpose of the exercises for men and women which follow. These exercises will help our readers reach the goal they all share: to become superb sex objects. After all, if we are not sex objects, what are we?

1. PUSH-UPS (Men)

Do this exercise in the nude. It is designed to make you an outstanding performer in the Missionary Position. True, push-ups make the man appear rather foolish to onlookers, but the benefits outweigh the temporary loss of face. If, however, you feel that doing push-ups alone is too undignified, you may place an obliging woman underneath you.

2. PUSH-DOWNS (Women)

Do this exercise in the nude. It is the classic push-up adjusted to the female sex. Assuming the same position as in the male push-up, the woman should then push *down* with the pelvic region, leaving the chest and torso as immobile as possible. The purpose of this exercise is to train women to assume the superior position in sex, that is, astride the man (*chevalade*). It is good to do this exercise to music. We suggest Von Suppe's "Light Cavalry Overture."

3. PANTING (Men and Women)

Do this exercise in the nude. Stand facing the north, hands at your side, shoulders back, tongue hanging out. Pant five times to the north. Then pant five times to the east, south, and west. Within a few weeks' time you should be able to pant ten times in each direction. After a few months you will run this figure up to twenty-five and you will be able to pant to the northeast and southwest. Now you are ready to pant lying down.

Lie nude on your bed or some other smooth surface, and pant straight up. Then turn your head and pant to the left, then to the right.

Do this exercise regularly. When next you are in a position to pant at your loved one, try your best to turn red in the face. Your partner will interpret this flush as an earnest of your love.

4. BUMP AND GRIND (Men and Women)

Do this exercise in the nude. Anyone who has ever seen a burlesque show is familiar with this body-builder. Rotate the hips in a full circle ten times clockwise and ten times counterclockwise. Encourage yourself by muttering, "Sir (or Madam), your engine is running." After completing the last rotation, put your hands in back of you just above the buttocks, and shoot the pelvis forward, accompanying this action with a loud grunt. If you are in the presence of friends, they may oblige by hitting the rim of your drum with a stick the moment your pelvis shoots forward. If you are without a drum, think seriously of adding one to your sex kit.

5. MOUTH AND TONGUE EXERCISE (Men)

Do this exercise in the nude. Buy a rubber bottle nipple and an aureole. They are available in your local breast-parts store. If the new aureole is a little rich for your blood, you can rent one by the hour or lease it on a long-term basis for tax purposes. Blow up a balloon and mount the aureole on it. Then paste the nipple in the center of the aureole. Throw the balloon in the air and as it comes down keep your hands behind your back and try to catch it by the nipple, using only your mouth. This trains you for accuracy in tongue-and-mouth work.

The aureole in this exercise is purely for ballast.

6. TONGUE EXERCISE (Men)

Do this exercise in the nude. Take another bottle nipple in your mouth. Using your tongue alone, rotate the nipple 45° to the left, return it to the normal position, and then rotate it 45° to the right. Begin by repeating this five times. In a few weeks you should be able to do this exercise twenty-five times in one session. Warning: this is

not a good exercise for men who are still hopping mad because they were weaned.

7. TONGUE EXERCISE (Women)

Do this exercise in the nude. It will give you excellent control when you indulge in oral sex. Insert a frankfurter into your mouth and practice biting on it as hard as you can *without breaking the skin.* This is a control exercise and you will find that you will have to lacerate many a weenie before you can exert just the proper amount of pressure. You may do the exercise with or without mustard, but never with sauerkraut. Sauerkraut beclouds the issue.

Women with small lovers may substitute Tootsie Rolls.

8. TONGUE EXERCISE (Men and Women)

Do this exercise in the nude. It is simple but effective and you can do it at home, in the office, or at social gatherings. Simply throw your head back and try to catch flies with your tongue. Devote a few months to this exercise and you will soon have the fastest tongue in your social circle, and you will be able to perform fellatio or cunnilingus when your love partner just happens to be passing by.

9. FEELIES (Men and Women)

Do this exercise in your clothes. You will need another person to act as Object. For this reason it is best done in a crowded elevator, where the Object cannot easily escape. The man selects an attractive woman on the elevator and squeezes his way next to her. He then feels her body all over, starting at the knees, up over the mons veneris, and to the breasts. The touch should be gentle but firm.

The woman who does the Feely should select a man

in the elevator, and she need not proceed above his testicles and penis.

This exercise is designed to increase tactile sensitivity. At times it is of great benefit to the Object as well as the person doing the exercise. At other times it is not.

If the Object expresses an adverse reaction, get off the elevator at the next floor. The speed of your departure will strengthen your legs and general muscle tone, and thus add to your sexual proficiency.

10. FEELIES (Men)

Do this exercise in the nude. Rub scented axle grease on your torso. Massage it gently into the armpits and around the pitiful nipples of the male breast. Be sure to rub a little into the delicate hollow at the base of your neck. When you are finished, towel yourself off with a maribou housecoat.

This exercise equips you to deal with the slippery situations you are bound to encounter in sexual couplings.

11. FEELIES (Women)

Do this exercise in the nude. Stretch out on the bed and spoon some *Sauce au Porto* into your navel.

For the sauce: First make two cups of standard brown sauce. Then boil half a cup of port wine in a saucepan until you have reduced it to about three tablespoons. Add the brown sauce and simmer for a few minutes. Take a sip to see if it needs more wine. If so, add port by the tablespoon. Simmer briefly. Then take three tablespoons of softened butter. Remove the sauce from the heat and beat in the butter, bit by bit. Let the sauce cool a little before spooning it into the navel.

Once it is in the navel, try to create a small clockwise whirlpool, using only the abdominal muscles. After you have mastered the clockwise whirlpool, start working on a counterclockwise whirlpool. Then remove the *Sauce au Porto* and set aside for dinner.

✗ 12. WEIGHT LIFTING (Men)

Do this exercise in the nude. Get your favorite book of pornography. Tie a string around a one-ounce weight. Tie the other end of the string to your penis, letting the weight rest on the floor. Be sure the string is not slack.

Now open your book of pornography and study the photographs until you begin to get an erection. Your aim in this exercise is to lift the one-ounce weight off the floor with your erection. Do not be discouraged if at first your penis can lift the weight only a quarter of an inch or so. In time you will be able to lift it five inches off the floor. Then graduate to a two-ounce weight. Your goal should be to lift a five-ounce weight with your erection. (Ferencz Zolny, of Hungary, lifted 9.4 ounces—a world's record—for which the Russians liquidated him during the Hungarian uprising.)

The benefits of this exercise are obvious, and if you work at it with determination you will develop a strong and forceful penis that will respond with alacrity whenever your sex partner calls upon it to fetch and carry.

13. BREAST-WINKING (Women)

Do this exercise in the nude. With intense mental concentration every woman can discover muscles whose existence she did not suspect. One such muscle lies beneath the aureole of each breast, and it enables women to contract the nipple until the skin folds over it, giving the appearance of a wink. Yussuf ibn Farad has testified that nothing excited him more than to see a nude woman turn her torso and wink at him provocatively with one of her breasts.

To achieve the breast wink lie on your bed or other appropriate surface, fold your hands behind your head, and stare lovingly at the ceiling. Now concentrate on one breast, repeating aloud as you do, "It *can* wink. It *can* wink. It *can* wink!"

Some women train both breasts, but since this exercise is rather exhausting, you should be quite content if one breast masters the wink.

14. RHYTHM EXERCISE (Men)

Do this exercise in the nude. Go to your record player and put on Beethoven's Fifth Symphony. Now conduct the symphony with your penis, grasping it firmly with only one hand. This exercise is most effective when you conduct with an erection, except during adagios. It helps develop that rhythmic sense so necessary to full mutual sexual satisfaction.

15. LABIAL VERBALIZATION (Women)

Do this exercise in the nude. Yes, it *is* true. You can talk with your labia. Like breast winking, labial conversation requires tremendous concentration and devotion, but the results are well worth it. Simply lie back on your bed, direct all your mental energies toward your labia, and implore them to speak. If you find it difficult, inspire yourself by looking forward to some breathtaking occasion when you can whisper a few labial nothings to your lover. His infinite delight and surprise will be ample reward for your efforts.

Start with a simple salutation such as "Hi, there," and then work your way up to full sentences. Progress will be slow but do not be discouraged. Remember Letitia

Graham, who, in her only public performance in Town Hall, November, 1973, gave a vaginal rendition of the "Bell Song" from *Lakme*.

Do you recall Olga Korbut, the little Russian gymnast who won the heart of the world during the 1972 Olympics? She achieved her astounding skill by training and exercising hour upon hour, day after day. Take the same approach to the sexual exercises listed here and you will soon find that you can reach heights of sensuality you thought were reserved only for Turks.

Strip and go to work *now*.

V
Orgasms and Other Noisemakers

For which would you sooner run over your grand-mother—a felon or an orgasm? The question answers itself. Orgasm is the goal, the ultima Thule, the Holy Grail, the pot of gold, the sizzle in the steak, the cream in your coffee, the lamb in your stew, the be-all and end-all of every lover's life. After a good orgasm there's really nothing you want to do next.

In early childhood most of us learn how to achieve that orgasm, usually by primitive manipulation of the sexual organs with our own fingers or those of a coopera-tive playmate. By the time we reach adulthood we have learned if we are sexually mature, to bring more variety into the process that ends in sexual climax. Tongue and lips applied to the penis or the clitoral area, the big toe enmeshed in the vagina of choice, and then the sex act itself, all lead down the glory road to that sensation of which Yussuf ibn Farad has written, "Makes you feel good all over."

The orgasm has a generally beneficent effect on the entire body. It improves digestion and skin and muscle tone, cures split hair ends, and lowers the cholesterol level.

The toes contract and the colon relaxes like a tired kitten. The tongue lies limp in aimless but delicious languor.

For those women who induce male orgasm via the primrose path of fellatio, it is cheering to learn that semen is high in polyunsaturated fats and low in calories.

Men, in general, can achieve orgasm in only one way: by determined manipulation of the penis. Women, however, hold the high cards in this game, especially if they are truly sensual and devoted to obtaining the very best their genitalia have to offer. A wise and knowing man, familiar with every erotic response of his partner, can bring her to orgasm many times before actual penile penetration by calling on "mother's little helpers"—the coke bottle, vibrator, electric toothbrush, shower spray, or rolling pin.

One case (and it is not unusual) involves a young woman whose lover knows precisely how sensitive are her breasts. He exposes them, kisses them gently, sucks on the nipples, and offers them extravagant compliments. Then he stops toying with them and talks to them seriously for a half hour or so. During this period the right breast is quiet and relaxed and the left breast is all ears. The left breast then responds by winking at him. In return, he whispers sweet nothings to it in their secret language of love (Basque). This brings the young woman to a raucous climax that scares hell out of the neighbors.

We have on record another woman whose *hallux,* or big toe, is maddeningly sensitive to pressure. Ordinary well-fitted shoes bring her to orgasm in a matter of seconds, and she has been forced to wear open-toed sandals except around the house, where her husband, an understanding man, is accustomed to her climactic gibberish. During sexual intercourse she leaves her shoes on.

Another woman achieves orgasm whenever she has lunch in a restaurant. Tests have proved that it is not the food that brings her to climax, but the mere fact of eating out. By the time she has coffee and dessert she has settled into a postcoital torpor, and she tips very well.

Orgasm, as we all know, is a phenomenon that deprives us of conscious control, and as such it can be dangerous. Many an apparently unmotivated murder takes place because orgasm deprived the killer of his normal mastery of the voluntary muscles. For this reason copulation should never occur when either of the lovers is bearing arms. People also scratch each other a lot during orgasm, even when neither partner complains of an itch. Many a young man has unwittingly bitten off the earlobe of his beloved while in the grip of orgasm. In the year 1974 one metropolitan hospital treated 367 women who had lost their earlobes to Cupid. Most of them claimed to have "walked into a doorknob."

Our records tell of a highly sexual woman who bit off her husband's nose during orgasm. He swore out a warrant for her arrest and took her to court on a charge of malicious mischief. During the trial the judge asked her to step into his chambers with her attorney for a conference. The judge, Charles Theodore Harmon, and the young woman's lawyer now answer to the soubriquet "No-Nose."

After orgasm a man generally needs R. & R. before he is capable of a new erection and a second orgasm. (Boys get an erection at the age of fourteen and it doesn't go away until the age of twenty-three.) In later years the period of R. & R. must be extended. Women, however, are capable of orgasm until exhaustion. Some of these orgasms are serial in nature. Compare them to a field of twenty runners in a one-mile race. The winner breaks the tape. Bunched up behind him are the second-, third-, and fourth-place runners, who break the tape almost, but not quite, simultaneously. Then the field straggles. First one and then

another runner breaks the tape. Finally, the last runner in the field stumbles across the finish line, and the lady is pooped. But give her a glass of milk and a cookie, and she is ready for the starter's gun once more.

Other women are capable of the sustained orgasm. Again, if we use our comparison of the twenty runners in a one-mile race, the runners are now holding hands as they cross the finish line. And she is still pooped.

It is this second or sustained orgasm that sexologists are trying to develop into the Permanent Orgasm. The work proceeds slowly, but from here and there come signs that we are on our way to success. Perhaps the most heartening record we have to date is that of a woman who began her orgasm on Guy Fawkes Day, 1965, and is still going strong out in Minneapolis even though her twenty-third lover has moved to Seattle and she lives on intravenous feedings.

Some unfortunate women, while they claim to enjoy the sex act, are incapable of reaching orgasm. This is seldom due to physiological difficulties. Usually such women have grown up in households where they were taught that sex is "dirty." To enjoy sex, therefore, is to enjoy something "dirty." Sometimes a wise psychological counsellor can help by pointing out that while sex can be clean, honest, open, and beautiful, maybe Yussuf ibn Farad was right when he said, "Sex is dirty, and I wouldn't have it any other way." Is a mature adult really interested in good clean fun?

Just as efficacious as a psychological counsellor is a tender and sensitive man who is understanding and patient. Our records include those of a woman who never reached orgasm although she married three men (serially), all of whom excited her physically. After her third marriage failed because of her sexual difficulties she met a young man to whom she told her problems. He was a university professor of geology with a fine career ahead of him, and he spent his sabbatical bringing her to orgasm. Since then she has remained in bed, where she plans to stay until his next sabbatical. He is, by the way, a specialist in igneous rock.

Men should always be cognizant of the greatly varying speed of response in women. By way of contrast to the woman and her young professor, other women respond so quickly that they often do not have time to take off their clothes. For such women dressing is a waste of time.

In men difficulties come not from slow but from too rapid response. This is known as "premature ejaculation." It amounts to jumping off the train before it reaches the station. But the word "premature" is a tricky one, and we must ask, "Premature in relation to what?"

To pin the word down, let us imagine a man in bed. The doorbell rings. He gets out of bed, walks downstairs and to the front door, flings it open, and finds himself face to face with King Kong, who is standing on the threshold. If the man then cries, "Oh, my God!" that is not a premature ejaculation. If, however, the doorbell rings and the man cries, "Oh, my God!" before getting out of bed, walking downstairs, and opening the door, that is indeed premature ejaculation. "Oh, my God!" is a response that should be reserved for the appearance of King Kong, not uttered for the mere ringing of the doorbell. Think of women in these terms and you will be better able to control your orgasm.

Just as compassionate men can assist women who have difficulty in reaching orgasm, so can compassionate women help solve the problem of premature ejaculation. Among our case histories is that of a woman whose husband was a two-minute man. For the first year of her marriage she made do by various stratagems. She toyed with dildoes, feather dusters, the vacuum cleaner, Italian sausage (sweet and hot), and summer squash, then switched to her husband for the home stretch. But she did not find satisfaction in all this. Somehow she missed the element of total sharing. And so she decided to help her husband overcome his problem.

Her method was simple and ingenious. After some forty seconds of coitus she excused herself to go to the kitchen because she thought she smelled gas. She returned to bed, assured her husband that the gas burners were off, and recommenced coitus. Thirty seconds later she excused herself again because a noise in the hall distracted her and she was afraid of a prowler. Naturally, the husband insisted on going himself to investigate. While he was out of bed she treated herself to a few whammies from the cordless vibrator. Then he returned to announce that the hall was clear. Already twelve minutes had gone by and her husband had not yet ejaculated! Another twenty seconds of coitus and she slipped out of bed to wash a sweater and take the curlers out of her hair. After her return to bed, she abandoned her usual position and rested on her hands and knees while offering her husband a rear entry (*crevissade*). It was in this position that a gnawing hunger overcame her, and she excused herself to make a bacon and tomato sandwich on white toast (hold the mayo!).

By such simple methods, and with the knowledge that tenderness and understanding can solve all the problems of love, she has now brought her husband to the point where it takes him six hours, with one fifteen-minute coffee break, to reach orgasm. And she is one happy bird!

Another aspect of orgasm that deserves discussion is the racket it makes. At the moment of climax the pupils of the eyes dilate, the fingernails curl inward, the navel rotates counterclockwise, and some people grow hair on their teeth. Vocal sounds, sometimes intelligible, sometimes not, accompany all these phenomena. Women are far more orgasmically vocal than men. They often cry out in sentences that parse nicely and are devoid of dangling participles, while men usually content themselves with stone-age howls and groans. Earlobe biters are silent, but that is because they cannot grunt with their mouths full.

The orgasm was not always as fully vocal as it is today. During the Victorian era women suffered under the delusion that sex brought no pleasure to the female. Prince Albert, Queen Victoria's consort (stud), bellowed like a Teutonic bull, whereas Victoria herself emitted only two regal squeaks at the moment of climax. In those days only a wanton would squeak thrice. More emboldened women of the era sometimes cried, "Fiddlesticks!" and then apologized profusely.

Today, when we have finally dispelled backward ideas of sexuality, the modern woman happily gives vent to whatever cries and sentiments, noble or otherwise, her orgasm urges on her. These cries are as varied as the flora and fauna of the field, and as pretty. It is impossible to categorize them. We have on record a woman who, upon reaching orgasm, recites "Trees" by Joyce Kilmer. On one occasion her orgasm was so sustained that she finished the poem and immediately launched into Washington's Farewell Address.

One couple, each of whom is musically endowed, mark their climax whenever it is simultaneous by singing the duet "La Ci Darem La Mano" from Mozart's *Don Giovanni*. It is not at all unusual for women of religious persuasion, giving themselves over to the body's ultimate pleasure, to recite the catechism. Others speak in tongues. Still others shout till the rafters ring or list the names of their lovers and other friends in alphabetical order. And according to Yussuf ibn Farad, "You haven't lived if you haven't heard a shepherdess come in Aramaic."

No one should under any circumstances attempt to censor or cut short the orgasmic cries. They are a delicious part of the pleasure of love. It often adds spice to the moment to call out lots of dirty words. One Quaker gentleman of our acquaintance finds himself shouting, despite his usually reticent nature, "I'm going to fuck thee to death!"—to which his spouse always responds, "Thou and who else?"

The next time you reach your climax remember to make lots of noise. Your partner will receive it as a tribute.

Every woman knows that at times she must be philanthropic with her body. Moments will come when her lover is obviously eager, and even though she feels tired and disinclined she will not want to disappoint him. Women's burdens are many and often the cares of the day are too onerous to allow of the delights of the night. Historical records tell us, for instance, that the late Mrs. Johann Sebastian Bach preferred to avoid sexual encounters when the children, Wilhelm Friedeman, Carl Phillip Emmanuel, Johann Gottfried Barnhard, Elisabeth Juliana Friedericke, Johann Christoph Friedrich, Johann Christian, Wilhelm Adolph, Gotthilf Wilhelm, Friedericke Sophia, Johann August, Johann Sebastian, Anna Carolina Phillipina, Johann Sebastian Altnikol, Anna Phillipina Friedericke, Wilhelm Friedrich Ernst, and Dorothea Charlotte Magdalena, had a cold.

Should Johann Sebastian Bach appear aroused at such times, Mrs. Bach obliged him despite her physical disinclination. Modern women often make this sacrifice as well, considering it a small price to pay to keep the enduring affection of a loved one. It is then that the wise woman will pretend an orgasm. She cannot, of course, duplicate the involuntary responses of the muscular system, the dilation of the pupils, the counterclockwise rotation of the navel, the inward growth of the fingernails, but she can and should tear her hair, shudder, and break out in the screaming meemies.

Be careful, however, to avoid the dangerous tendency to make the ersatz orgasm sound better than the real McCoy. If this should occur, your husband or lover will feel he has disappointed you on other occasions, when he is actually doing far better than usual. Confine your orgasmic cries to simple declarative sentences at such times. It is enough to shout, "Fort Sumter has fallen!" to convince your lover that he has brought you to a satisfying conclusion of your lovemaking.

VI

The Naked Ape: Our
Sexual Fantasies

Most women lead a rich erotic fantasy life as they go about their daily chores, cleaning and cooking and washing and comparing scouring powders. They fantasize alone and in friendly groups, but best of all, they fantasize during the act of coitus, when they are in the arms of their lovers. A woman will usually keep her fantasies to herself at such a time because her lover, busy as a bee as he strives to bring her to bliss, might be hurt to learn that nothing could be further from her mind than himself. How can a woman, teetering on the brink of climax, confess to her lover that he is playing second fiddle to an amorous warthog?

Yet why should men take such fantasies amiss? Is there a woman alive who has not, in the sweet and mindless combat of love, let her thoughts wander to her neighbor's Afghan hound or to Paul Newman?

Men, for some reason we do not yet understand, fantasize far more infrequently than women, and their fantasies are usually simple and to the point. During coitus the average male fantasizer closes his eyes and tries to think of a naked lady. As fantasies go, this does not amount to a hill of beans.

But while men fantasize less often than women, their fantasies can on occasion be extremely active. Some energetic and aggressive males close their eyes and think of as many as three hundred naked ladies. One male fantasizer, an agnostic whose grandfather was a full-blooded Cherokee, used to close his eyes and think of 850 naked ladies, but his case was unusual. Another man, in the process of completing a *crevissade,* fantasized that he was also performing cunnilingus upon a second woman and titillating the clitoris of a third, while with his free hand he clutched a squeegee and washed the windows. When the windows were clean he could observe across the courtyard a sexual bout involving two damsels, four swains, a cricket bat, a bottle of Budweiser, and a referee. The Budweiser was foaming, as would be expected in such a situation.

But well-developed male fantasies such as this are the exception. For this reason we are devoting this chapter exclusively to the female sexual fantasy. We have for two years been collecting female sexual fantasies door-to-door, offering one Naughty Marietta silver-plated place setting for each fantasy. A study of these fantasies indicates that income and education have little to do with the quality of the fantasy. Devout churchgoing women have, by and large, the same fantasies as atheists and agnostics, but they hear organ music in the background.

Here we present in the words of the fantasizer herself some of the most common and revealing female sexual fantasies.

1. (White Caucasian female, age 32)

"I am in bed with Frederick. During foreplay, I am aware only of him and his big toe, and I offer no resistance while he laps the marmalade off my instep. Only when he starts up with the dry ice does my mind begin to wander.

In the distance I hear a dog barking and I know it is Spot, my childhood pet, who chewed up my first brassiere. Then Frederick enters me. I close my eyes, and in my fantasy I am on the telephone, talking to my mother. I say, 'Look, ma, no hands!' and at that moment I experience a gloriously exciting orgasm. But Frederick has not yet climaxed because he is only halfway through the cookbook. He never comes until shellfish.

"Sometimes I vary this fantasy. I do not call my mother but the telephone rings anyway and when I answer it I am talking to the business office of the telephone company. The woman I am talking to is named Mrs. Peabody. We go over last month's bill, item by item. I fight over each item, and when Mrs. Peabody informs me that she is going to cut off my service, Frederick and I both begin serial orgasms."

2. (White Caucasian female, age 41)

"I begin my fantasy the moment my husband Gerard starts to pant. Gerard is an extremely skilled panter (he panted for the United States in the 1972 Olympics), and even when he pants at me over the telephone I have an immediate physical response. The long-distance pant, however, seldom triggers me to complete the fantasy. When Gerard is in bed with me, that is a horse of a different color.

"The horse is a chestnut roan, a former Kentucky Derby winner who has been put out to stud at $25,000 a boff. I imagine that I am in a lush meadow, grazing contentedly on all fours. Four nude men, two of whom are Paul Newman, approach me with ropes and tie me up. Then they carry me, trussed as I am, to a platform in the stable. They tie a feedbag on my face. As I nibble the oats the strawberry roan mounts me. When I complete this fantasy the satisfaction is unbelievable.

"Later, as I lie in bed with Gerard, I curry him gently. Because he is a good husband, he obliges me by whinnying at such moments.

"My fantasies, however, have had a very sad ending. Last week Gerard broke his leg and I had to shoot him."

3. (White Caucasian female, age 22)

"I have a favorite fantasy, which I enjoy during sex, shopping, sports, or other activities. The fantasy is so vivid that I can depend upon it to bring me to climax when I am all by myself or in the company of those near and dear to me.

"As I go about my business I imagine that I am walking through thick and verdant vegetation. Although I am dressed demurely, as is my custom, I am not wearing panties, as is also my custom. I come to a lovely tree. I climb it and sit in a fork, my knees up and my legs spread. Gently, I pluck leaves from the tree and tuck them into my vagina. Then I sit and wait.

"In anywhere from ten to fifteen minutes a giraffe comes by. The giraffe is worried because he has not been including enough greens in his diet. I satisfy the giraffe, and when he finally leaves me, it is with friendly feelings.

"Is this unusual? Should I be ashamed of my fantasy? I would tell my hubby about it but he doesn't like roughage."

4. (White Caucasian female, age 35)

"When Carl, my current lover, excites me in bed, I immediately slip off into a fantasy.

"Carl disappears and I make believe that a long line of naked men extends from my bed to the front door. The

men are well-behaved and no one tries to buck the line.

"I recognize everyone in the line. The regulars are Senator Jackson, Brezhnev, Henry Kissinger, that darling little Senator Baker, Hugh Scott, Bob Haldeman, and the President of the United States.

"Each penetrates me in turn and I grow increasingly excited, but I do not climax until Bob Haldeman gets up to let the President of the United States have his turn. After he penetrates me I begin an extended orgasm that lasts for the duration of the SALT talks.

"At this stage I open my eyes to discover that the President is Paul Newman. He tells me that he ran as an independent, and I bite his ear off.

"Since Carl, my lover, is two-eared, I know that I am only imagining things. I would tell Carl about my fantasy but he doesn't like me to mess around with politics."

5. (White Caucasian female, age 30)

"I usually have this fantasy during daylight hours but I sometimes have it week-nights also. (I go away weekends.)

"Peter comes into the room when I am doing the ironing. I hit him over the head with a baseball bat. Then, as he lies unconscious, I pause for a moment to admire him. I know that I am lucky in having Peter for a lover. It is not every man who can sustain an erection during a brain concussion. While he is still unconscious I handcuff his hands behind his back, put a ring through his nose, and then run a rope through the ring to the chandelier. Then I strip myself bare and run down to the dry cleaners. Max, the dry cleaner, waits on me. He holds a piece of marking chalk in his hand. It is about six inches long and three and a half inches in circumference. He tells me that my Givenchy suit is ready, and I climax.

"Max does French dry cleaning."

6. (White Caucasian female, age 41)

"I have always daydreamed about letting Wally, my lover, beat the shit out of me. Usually I imagine that he has pulled my panties down and he spanks me with a Ping-Pong paddle that has a sandpaper finish. In my fantasy, that begins to excite me, but I want Wally to hurt me even more. I ask him to exchange the Ping-Pong paddle for a delicious whip whose thongs end in pellets of bauxite. He does so, but I am still frustrated. I am at the edge of orgasm, but the edge recedes. I beg him to hit me on the jaw with a pair of brass knuckles. He finally agrees and he stuns me with a sharp right to the button. My chin bleeds and I faint, but I have a long and satisfying orgasm as I sink unconscious to the floor.

"I have known Wally for years. I have told him about my fantasy and it doesn't shock him because he is a serious student who has studied sex at the New School for Social Research. Wally is a supportive-type jock and an understanding one. Last week I implored him to help me live out my fantasy in reality. I had to get on my knees and kiss his feet, but he finally agreed. He paddled me and whipped me, and followed that with a hard right across to the jaw.

"The next time I see that sonofabitch I'm going to kill him."

7. (Purple mesomorphic female, aged 27)

"My father was in real estate. I have grown up to believe that the only true wealth is land. Maybe that explains why all my sexual fantasies are real-estate fantasies. I have many different kinds of real-estate fantasies, some involving uncleared acreage, others building developments or low-rise tax-payers.

"In my favorite fantasy, the one that never fails to bring me to a marathon orgasm, I am a large excavation in Manhattan. As I lie there, relaxed and open as only an excavation can be, the Empire State Building slowly fills me up. As I draw the building into myself, I feel incredible sensations from the express elevators, and when the building has its orgasm it floods me with mail from all the out-baskets.

"Later, as I moved toward group sex in my real life, I developed this fantasy further. I became an even larger excavation and I gave myself to the twin towers of the World Trade Center. I thought that this would double my pleasure, but it didn't work out that way because the twin towers are not fully rented.

"I am always actively striving to extend and develop my fantasy life. Right now I have an eye on some property in Vermont, and a parcel of land just outside Cooperstown, New York. Developers will soon be falling over each other to get their hands on that parcel. It is an ideal location for a horny shopping center.

"Speaking of horny, there's an awful lot of acreage in this great land of ours. Is it any wonder that I am a happy and fulfilled woman? God bless America!

"I am against real-estate taxes."

8. (White Caucasian female, age 19)

"I am a young virgin lying nude in a mossy glen. An armadillo slithers up to me and ravishes me. The experience is especially exciting because the armadillo is of a different faith."

9. (White Caucasian female, age 25)

"I am alone in my room at night, lying nude on the bed and studying myself in the ceiling mirror. Suddenly the wind rustles the curtains on my window. The window opens and a large naked black man steals into the room.

His penis is about ten inches long and adorned with the flag of one of the emergent African nations. He ties my hands and feet to the bedposts and rapes me. I should mention that he takes the flag off first.

"For a few moments I am furious with him, but the fury soon turns to tenderness. When I have my orgasm I know that I want him to steal into my room every night for the rest of my life. I am still tied up as he rises from the bed. I watch in amazement. Until that moment I had not known that Robert Redford was black."

10. (White Caucasian female, age 33)

"I am with Prince, my boyfriend. I am brought to full orgasm whenever Prince barks at Paul Newman, the mailman."

11. (White Caucasian female, age 27)

"I am a secretary and every day when the weather is clement I go to the park during my lunch hour to eat the sandwich and the piece of fruit I take with me to work. As soon as I sit down on the park bench I begin my fantasy.

"A man sits down next to me. He has a bad head cold and he is sniffling. He blows his nose unsuccessfully. I feel a pleasant tightening in my groin.

"A parks-department employee comes by. He has a long stick with a nail on the end of it, and with this implement he spears bits of paper and puts them in the burlap bag slung over his shoulder. At this very moment a woman pushes a baby carriage past me. The baby is crying. By now I am so moist that I am thinking of changing my panties.

"Then I look up and see a policeman writing out a parking ticket. I watch him carefully as he does. When he is finished, he affixes the ticket to the windshield wiper of a beautiful Stutz Bearcat. I feel my abdominal muscles contract and I have a loud orgasm that attracts no little attention among the cognoscenti in the park."

We hope that these representative examples of female sexual fantasies will encourage women to share them with their loved ones. Our fantasy life is an important means of communication, and sexual fantasies enrich the world of reality.

The Library of Congress would like to hear from women who have appealing sex fantasies. Send yours in today. The Library will catalog them so that they can be available to the general public.

VII
Venery Is for Two—
But Can We Say the Same
for Concupiscence?

We have written this book for an audience of people who, like Yussuf ibn Farad, have a full team of sexual partners plus a good bench upon whom to hone their skills in bringing off an aesthetically acceptable *croupade, chevalade, crevissade,* and *McSorley's Flannel Tongue-Lash.* Yet what of those among our readers whose genitalia are temporarily unemployed and who have not yet met someone who will respond wholeheartedly to the body's insatiable sexual demands? Perhaps our readers include women who have run out of lovers and must make do with a dildo in decorator colors, and men whose major urge is to be unfaithful to their artificial vaginas. These readers may be technically superb lovers and sensualists, but of what use is this expertise unless they meet accommodating people of the opposite sex, or even the same sex if they are in the mood to explore their raging bisexuality?

When men or women have suffered long periods of enforced continence their bodies give off signals that indicate they are profoundly interested in lovemaking. Their earlobes become moist. Another telltale sign is the growth of ingrown hairs around the Adam's apple. Sometimes sexually deprived women will simply lift their heads and shriek. The Arabs call this the *qabhi abba tufat,* or "love shriek," and it is considered ungallant not to pay attention to it.

As we discuss the techniques of meeting people, we start with one demotic problem. Women in the United States outnumber men. From this we draw an obvious conclusion: men must go around more.

Meeting lascivious people of the opposite sex is no problem once you overcome a natural timidity and fear of being kneed in the groin. You will find singles wherever you look: in singles bars, museums, at athletic events, in restaurants, on public conveyances, in church, at the frozen-food bin in the supermarket. Be you male or female, your attitude must be one of open and unashamed search. Everyone you meet should be able to read in your face that you are hormonal, adventurous, sexually bold, willing to try any and every new erotic sensation, impatient with your current state of celibacy, and yet a man or woman of taste who will not slip thoughtlessly into a relationship unless it gives promise not only of physical but also of psychological rewards. For this, of course, you will need a very large face. If you feel your face is at present too small to carry all these messages, try these two simple exercises: first, put an index finger in each corner of your mouth and pull hard, stretching the cheeks to their greatest potential. Repeat this exercise twenty-five times before going to bed and after brushing your teeth. This will stretch your face horizontally. The second exercise is the simple yawn. Yawn to full capacity twenty-five times each night. This will give your face the vertical stretch it needs. Only a fully stretched face can tell the whole story of your rampant sexuality to members of the opposite sex.

Whenever you are seeking a new sex partner, look around for those who appear to be alone, then make your assessment. Does he or she appear to be a sufficiently rapacious and voracious sex object? What does the face say to you? The body? The posture? Pay special attention to any single who is panting. Here you must make a subtle distinction between panting and being out of breath. The person who is out of breath is merely trying to inhale enough oxygen into his lungs so that his breathing may return to normal. A panter, however, is panting not because he or she wants to return to normal breathing, but because that person wants to pant with a member of the opposite sex.

Yussuf ibn Farad often wandered through the fields in search of a quickie to while away the idle hour, and he always stopped to admire a sheep before he transferred his attentions to the shepherdess. You can learn from Yussuf. When you walk through your local park you may encounter very few people airing their sheep, but dogs will be plentiful. If you see a member of the opposite sex holding a leash with a dog on the end of it, stop to admire the dog. Stroke its fur gently. Call attention to how the dog shudders in delight under your touch. Remark on what fine legs it has. If the dog is a bitch you might say a few words about her splendid bosom. If the dog is male it will not be inappropriate to remark what a well-hung beast he is. Hold the dog's muzzle and comment on the sensuous canine lips. All this will ingratiate you to the dog's owner, who will not take it amiss when you raise your eyes from the dog's rump to the human counterpart.

Instill into yourself an all-out attitude in your quest for a sexual mate and you will soon realize that men and women can approach each other in any situation, any location, under any circumstances. Conquer the impulse to rub up against a potential lover. That will come later. Both men and women prefer to begin a relationship with words. A vocal approach is the first step.

Suppose you are a woman on a bus. At the next stop

a relatively hairless Swede gets on and takes his place among the strapholders. You appraise him carefully. He is above medium height, of splendid build, quite blond, high forehead, and with full lips not usually associated with Scandinavians. He appeals to you at first glance, and even more so when you observe that his left hand is making slight adjustments in his pants pocket. But wait! Do not be too impetuous. Ask yourself whether you want an involvement with a man who obviously does not have to shave every day. Can you get along comfortably with so little body hair? When you reach the stage of sexual experimentation and play, are you really willing to tolerate smorgasbord in your vagina?

Let us say the answer to all these questions is affirmative and you want to pursue a relationship with the Oaf of Stockholm. How to go about it? You might move close to him in the bus, hold firmly to a strap with one hand, and give him a sharp kick in the ass. This will startle him and he will turn to you. Now you are in a position to do something that always brings people closer together. You can offer him a gracious apology and explain that you mistook him for your mother. He will accept your apology. Then you casually tell him that you have just returned from your deep Hawaiian cream massage, and ask what *he* does for relaxation. From there on in it should be easy sailing no matter how chill the waters off Sweden's shores.

This approach has an added advantage. Now and then you will discover a man whom a sharp kick in the ass stimulates sexually. Then your only problem will be how to get off the bus in time.

Before you start your opening verbal ploy to engage the attentions of a member of the opposite sex, give careful thought to the time, the place, and the circumstances. The approach will not be the same in the museum as in Shea Stadium. What might be appropriate to murmur in front of the onion bin in the green grocer's might be highly out of place in the ladies' room at St. Stephen's.

When opening a conversation with a highly desirable stranger, try to give as much pertinent information about yourself as possible. If you are a man, you might begin by saying, "My name is George Marran. I am in an upper income bracket, working as a management consultant in the quick-foods industry, and my marital status is in doubt. It might also interest you to know that I have both psoriasis and an erection. How do you do?"

An opener such as this will tell your new-found friend exactly where you stand in life, and it is sure to elicit a response.

Let us assume that you are a man who wants to meet someone he has spied in cultural surroundings. You are attending a performance of *A Midsummer Night's Dream,* and you go to the lobby during the first intermission. There, beneath a portrait of Maude Adams playing Peter Pan in the nude, is a young woman of antic cleavage and sloe eyes, her earlobes moist, her lips slightly open as she pants delicately, her décolleté dress revealing just a hint of bauxite brassiere. You are encouraged, especially when you notice that she is slipping a rolled program up the inside of her dress. You might approach her in such wise:

YOU

Dear lady, though I am a stranger, seeing
you thus in your wonted liveries, I am
waggishly impelled to suggest that we
might be not misgraffed.

This will grab her by the short hair, and she might respond:

SHE

'Twould be fond of me to make pageant
of disinterest when your manly savors
bespeak not the lob.

Hearing this, you might immediately press your advantage and ask for her phone number. If she agrees, she is clearly willing to suffer you a date, during which you will have the opportunity to explore each other. But a decent temperance should impel you not to importune too rashly at this juncture. Perhaps you should take her to the Museum of Modern Art, or go with her on a shopping trip and help carry her fardels home. Then, after two dates during which you establish the basis for the relationship, you may safely strike at her nearest erogenous zone.

In any case, boldness and a determination to do homage to Venus are all the prospective lover needs in his search for companionship.

What if a stranger makes advances and the advances are not welcome? Remember that the urge that prompted the advance is love, and therefore no one should brush off another human being in an inconsiderate or hurtful fashion. A young woman, for instance, who seeks to turn aside the obvious sexual approach of an anthropoid middle linebacker for the New York Jets might turn to him and emit a distinct but ladylike belch. But middle linebackers are notoriously difficult to discourage, and if he proves obstinate the young woman should choose her words carefully and murmur, "Fuck off." This will usually accomplish its purpose and with no ill feelings on either side.

Given the social conventions governing the commerce between the sexes, it is more difficult for men to brush off women, and less likely to be taken in good grace. One ploy that usually works well is for the man to tell the woman he wishes to brush off that he is a spy from the Benedictine order wearing mufti so that he might more easily swipe a brandy recipe from Courvoisier. This will give him a certain *cachet* in her eyes, as well as an acceptable excuse for rejecting the blandishments of his Aphrodite. If, however, she has come across two or three other Benedictine monks on leave during the past week, the man will be in trouble. In this case it might be safer, and certainly more efficacious, for him to confess to trench mouth.

When seeking a lover remember to avoid all mannerisms, mode of dress, and conditions that tend to cool rather than heighten passion. No one wants a lover who has matted chewing gum in the hair. Old sneakers do not encourage lubricity, and foul breath ne'er won fair maid. High on the list of sexual "turn-offs" is Hansen's Disease, more commonly known as leprosy. We no longer hold to medieval and rather cruel superstitions about this disease. We know that it can be cured and that it is not contagious. Yet prejudice continues to exist, and if you have Hansen's Disease it is best to clear it up before making sexual advances.

Look for a lover who shares at least some of your major interests. If you are an avid collector of pre-Columbian jockstraps, surely somewhere you will find a man or woman who shares this passion. Perhaps your hobby is picking your nose. Indulge it in public and sooner or later some kindred and sexually compatible soul will comment on your skill and technique. In this country alone we have millions of nose-pickers who want nothing more than to come out of the closet.

You have met someone. You are about to set out together on the beautiful path of sensual love. But perhaps your new lover is shy and psychologically repressed no matter how physically aroused. Be patient. Gradually lead your partner into the experimentation that is so much a part of a fully realized sexual life. Do you recall the motion picture *Blanket and Bed?* Remember how long it took the Kansas City pederast in that picture to bring Mitzi Morgan to her senses.

It may be better, before you start actual intercourse,

to sit down with your new acquaintance and make a list of the things you each like to do sexually. The *Kerry-Down-Derry*? The half *Soixante-Neuf*, or *Trente-Quatre et Demi*? *Apple Brown Betty*? Then strike from the list whatever either partner objects to. Now you have a meeting of the minds. Tack the list on the wall behind the bed, and begin.

If you yourself are hesitant and timid in beginning a new relationship, you can do no better than to recall the words of Yussuf ibn Farad, "Fucking is a great way to break the ice."

VIII
The Doughnuts of
Aphrodite

Early in the sixteenth century Juan Ponce de León governed the island of Puerto Rico. Ponce considered the *droit du seigneur* a shining example of participatory democracy, and he divided his time between robbing the island blind and deflowering indigenous damsels.

As he neared the end of his governorship, in 1512, he grew depressed and fell victim to a form of cyclothymia. Behold Ponce, a man whose passions had often driven him to adorable excesses, lying abed, arms folded behind his head, eyes on the ceiling, painfully aware of the quivering and nubile islander who lay next to him in the buff. The young thing obviously expected from the Governor that which he was suddenly unable to provide. Ponce's spirit still bayed at the moon, but his flesh was all tuckered out. He tried to flay his body into some semblance of sexual response. He got down on his hands and knees to blow on the dying embers of his former raptures. Nothing availed, and so Ponce set forth to discover a fountain of youth whose pure waters would prove to be the primordial aphrodisiac.

Ponce pursued the quest in Florida, the land he discovered, until he came upon a passel of Indians who were sexually tireless and well adjusted. Ponce's study of the tribe convinced him that its members imbibed their sexual gusto with the Florida spring water they drank. Taking off his helmet, Ponce dipped it into the tribe's spring and drank a long and satisfying draught. Then he sat down and patiently waited for an erection.

While he was waiting, the Indians cut the poor bastard to ribbons. Alas, Ponce never knew that this tribe, the Weepasaukee, was notoriously chintzy about handing out free drinking water to any hirsute Iberian who happened to wander by.

So much for Ponce. And so much for Florida, where today hordes of gamey geriatrics carry on in his spirit.

Was there such a thing as a fountain of youth? Do aphrodisiacs in the form of food or drink which encourage venery and improve sexual performance actually exist? Is Spanish fly nothing more than a maiden's prayer? Is the rumor about oysters true, or is it only the result of an all-too-human urge to say something nice about shellfish?

The answer to all these questions is equivocal. Aphrodisiacs exist, and in abundance, but they do not induce an automatic sexual response. Yet, in the words of Yussuf ibn Farad, "A little crushed eye of newt never hurt anyone." Other popular aphrodisiacs are mandrake root, powdered rhinoceros horn, and Alka Seltzer, all available at your local supermarket.

A large regional power failure is also an aphrodisiac, because in our modern society the lack of power forces leisure upon us. When a man and a woman are together without light, radio, or television, they are left with only one thing to do, unless, of course, they are content to sit in the dark and fiddle around with their inner lives.

An aphrodisiac will work only if the lover acquires it in the proper manner and uses it in a prescribed way. Its incorrect use will pay no more sexual dividends than a bowl of grapenuts. (This is intended in no way to de-

tract from Neustadt's landmark biological discovery that the male grape has nuts.)

Consider the ginseng root. Lovers, by and large, acknowledge without question the aphrodisiac properties of ginseng. Yet although it is a simple matter to brew and imbibe an acceptable ginseng tea, the disappointed lover may find that the ginseng has had no appreciable effect on his or her libido. Why? Probably because the lover did not obtain the ginseng in the proper fashion.

Obtaining ginseng is not quite as simple as it may appear. Researchers estimate that over 480,000 cities and towns in the United States suffer from a severe ginseng shortage, a scandalous situation which our largely frigid government agencies have taken no steps to rectify. Obviously the Administration cares not one whit that ginseng exists only in those large urban centers that boast a substantial Oriental community. Needless to say, such communities guard jealously what little stores of ginseng they possess.

If you, the lover, are male, you will first have to insinuate yourself into your local Oriental community, possibly through political connections, the use of personal influence, or plastic surgery. Then, when you locate the ginseng outlet, you must make your purchase in such a manner as to guarantee the magic root's aphrodisiac efficacy.

Buy your ginseng only from a moist and naked Chinese maiden. Come armed with Scotch tape. Ask the maiden to take the ginseng root and break it in half. Tape one half of the ginseng root just above the nipple of the naked maiden's left breast, and tape the other half in the same location on the right breast. Then, with your hands behind your back, remove the ginseng with your lips and teeth, first from one breast, then from the other. Drop the two halves of the ginseng into the pan of boiling water which should be at hand. While you are doing this, you might ask the Chinese maiden if she would be kind enough to apply a little soya sauce (another aphrodisiac) to your penis and stroke it gently but firmly.

You have brewed your ginseng tea, and the moment you swallow your first sip you will find yourself in a state of fierce and burning sexual desire.

If you, the lover, are female, simply reverse the roles. Buy your ginseng from a young, naked, well-proportioned Chinese lad. Strip and let him tape a piece of ginseng to each of your breasts. While he retrieves the pieces of ginseng with the labial technique described above (with the understanding that you are still the rightful owner of the valuable root), anoint his penis with soya sauce and stroke it gently but firmly. You will shortly discover that the ginseng tea is every bit as effective for women as for men.

Hundreds of foods are aphrodisiacs if the lover ingests them in the proper manner. Here we have space for only a few of the more common and easily accessible ones. The true aphrodisiac works equally on the passions of either sex.

Few people realize what exquisite erotic sensations the ordinary doughnut can inspire, because they use it ill. Let us say at once that dunking a doughnut in coffee immediately dissipates its potential for sexual excitation, because of the chemical reaction between starch and caffeine. To get the full benefit of a doughnut's aphrodisiac potential a woman should hold it parallel to the floor and grasp it between the thumb and third finger while the lover at her side lies nude on his back. Then she should gently slip the doughnut down the shaft of her lover's erect penis. (If his penis is not erect it is important for her to change lovers quickly or the doughnut will go to waste). The woman should now recline on her left side, her left elbow crooked and her head resting on her left hand, her right arm cushioned against her lover's buttocks. In this position she should slowly and languorously nibble the doughnut until it is all gone, and then lap up whatever crumbs may be lying around. (The napkin should be placed on the left). Where are the sexual partners who could fail to find a doughnut, thus employed, sexually stimulating?

In ethnic situations the lovers may favor a bagel over the doughnut. In fact, the aphrodisiac qualities of the bagel last longer than those of the doughnut.

Ordinary cow's milk also has the properties of a first-rate aphrodisiac. Lie face down (we are assuming nudity) on your bed. Let your sex partner pour a little milk into the small of your back, and then place two fluffy kittens next to the milk. For best results, deny the kittens food and drink for three days prior to the act.

Over the centuries mankind has found that the range of aphrodisiacs approaches the infinite. To prove this point the male can make a simple experiment that costs little in time or money. All he needs is an affable woman and a jar of lowly peanut butter. Apply a thin coating of peanut butter to the clitoris of your beloved, and slowly lap it off. You will discover that peanut butter possesses attributes of which you never dreamed.

And is it not carrying coals to Newcastle to remind everyone that a banana, taken vaginally, is a time-tested aphrodisiac for women?

But the greatest aphrodisiac of all is not a commodity. It is the feeling one has toward one's sexual partner. The name of that feeling—and mark it well—is "unbridled lust." As Yussuf ibn Farad has said, "Unbridled lust is the only path to true love."

Will our male readers forgive us if we quote once more from the master, Yussuf? "Whenever my passions lag," he wrote, "I rub myself down thoroughly with a young woman."

IX

The Tie-dyed Penis

Foreplay, coitus, fantasy, masturbation, all aspects of love, have evolved from mankind's past. A study of that past helps us to better understand the present and to equip ourselves to be more accomplished sex partners. A steady line leads from Yussuf ibn Farad's invention of foreplay to the modern double-dipped dildo.

When we turn to anthropology for a study of our erotic past we discover that we are but a chapter in the sexual history of mankind, and our children will continue the story, day and night. By learning how primitive sex customs led us to our present state of radiant sexuality, we will be able better to predict what forms sexual activity will take in the future. We would be blind indeed, and not a little vainglorious, if we believed that in the *Punjab Twist* and *Willy's Wheelbarrow* sex had reached its apotheosis. Unseen Everests await our discovery and conquest.

For a study of the past we rely mainly on a scientific examination of those peoples we call "previbrates," people whose culture is still that of the Pre-Vibrator age.

We go first to the Mambiti, who inhabit a small unnamed island east of Bora Bora. There we find a peaceful people making the best use they can of their previbrate technology. The Mambiti are gentle, almost childlike, and since they subsist on a diet of fish and fresh fruit, enough of which they can gather in an hour's time to take care of the day's nutritional requirements, they spend their idle hours in various sexual activities. Mambiti men and women are extremely fond of sexual ornamentation. The women, from the age of puberty, content themselves with applying henna to the labia. Those with more pronounced clitorises usually adorn them with tiny floral wreaths known as "futahetoa." A girl who can wear three or even four futahetoa on her clitoris is a very proud Mambiti indeed, and her bride price will be one of the highest on the island.

In addition, Mambiti maidens and women often part their pubic hair. Virgins wear the part on the left, nonvirgins on the right.

After the age of twelve, when every boy is considered a man, he will tie his penis in a simple slipknot and dip it in various vegetable dyes. As with the futahetoa, the boy who can tie more than one knot in his penis before dipping it in the dyes wins himself a respected place in the community and all nubile girls will seek him out. After the dyes have dried and the young man has untied his penis, the effect is rather like a post-office mural.

A Mambiti male will often encase his penis in banana peels, a form of play. The Mambiti lass, upon seeing this, will know that the man wants her to take part in an island game and to "make hatitoe," that is, to "peel" his penis. Perhaps it is for this reason that the banana has become a universal sex symbol, accounting for the crazed sexual activities that take place on every banana boat.

On a neighboring island, the Tamitata share many of the customs of the Mambiti plus a few that are peculiar to their tribal society. One of these concerns the "titawuwu," or love-whistle, which the fathers carve for the girl children of the island on the day of their birth. The father of the newborn girl-child buries the titawuwu in a secret place, usually beneath a flowering bougainvillea tree, awaiting the day when his daughter reaches maturity. The Tamitata consider the girl mature two minutes after her first menses. At that moment, the father goes to the secret hiding place, digs up the titawuwu, or love-whistle, and hands it to the girl. She runs with it to the top of Kalahinani, the highest mountain on the island, where she blows the whistle all day long to let the young men of the tribe know that she is ready. The piercing sound of the titawuwu can carry as far as ten miles and it always attracts a crowd. Although considerably distorted in meaning today, the phrase "blowing the whistle on someone" has come to us from this custom.

Turning to less inviting climes and more austere conditions, where the rigors of life do not permit of much sexual dalliance, we next look at the Eskimo. As most of us know, an Eskimo hunting trip may keep the men away from the village for many weeks. Before the men leave, the women of the village wail and moan to protest their abandonment. In order to stifle these unseemly cries, the Eskimo men freeze their women in a block of ice. If the hunt is successful and the tribe has temporarily solved its food problem, the men begin thawing out their women by rubbing the ice blocks with hot blubber. This is considered foreplay. When they finally reach the women, they have tired of foreplay and proceed at once to the Eskimo fashion of penetration, which is quick and to the point.

If the hunt is unsuccessful, the women remain in their ice blocks until the next hunt has concluded. Eskimo women have been known to remain in their ice blocks through as many as five hunts, but they are usually of

little use after that, and the men send them to Nome to carve seals for the souvenir shops. It is significant that today we still speak of "thawing out" a cold woman.

On the Melanesian island of Tana-Lanua courtship ritual is of particular interest to the student. The Tana-Lanuans weave an amazingly soft cloth out of palm fibers, and they have relatively sophisticated methods of dyeing the cloth various colors. When a girl reaches the age of fourteen it is time for her to select a sex partner. All the boys of fifteen or older line up before the Love Hut and dance about while the girls watch. Each girl carries a blue ribbon made of the palm-fiber cloth. At exactly high noon, the elder of the tribe blows the Tana-Lanuan version of the titawuwu, whereupon each girl races for the boy of her choice and ties the blue ribbon around his scrotum. This ribbon is a signal to other girls that he is "taken" and not available. If a girl makes an approach to a ribboned boy who is not her own, she is put into protective custody for one month and forced to comb her pubic hair straight back.

Sometimes two girls will reach the same boy at once, and both will tie blue ribbons around his scrotum. In a good year the tribe may have as many as twelve two-ribbon boys, and perhaps even a three-ribbon boy or two.

After the courtship reaches the stage of marriage (a boy may marry as many girls as he has ribbons), the ribbons remain. During the little quarrels that are common to all marriages the girls will sometimes tighten the ribbon. But if the marriage is an unhappy one and both partners want to end it in the Tana-Lanuan version of divorce, the process is simplicity itself. Using an instrument somewhat akin to the machete, the wife will sever the blue ribbon. As it drops to the ground the husband becomes eligible again and waits for another maiden to bedeck his scrotum. If the divorce is bitter and acrimonious, the husband often whimpers in fright when the time comes for his wife to seize the machete and cut the ribbon.

We can see how this custom has survived in our modern ritual of cutting a ribbon before opening a new bridge or tunnel.

Along the shores of the Amazon in Brazil lives a tribe of previbrates called the Orunami. It is instructive to follow in detail a typical Orunami courtship. An attractive Orunami girl walks from the Short House to the Medium House and then to the Long House. In the course of her stroll her appearance attracts the attention of a young man who cannot keep the ritual liana vines from slipping off his erect penis. Once she passes the Long House, he leaps out from behind the Medium House, brushes the foliage aside, and pants three times. She immediately lies down on the ground and allows him to penetrate her at once, using the Missionary Position. After coitus, they both murmur endearments and caress each other's bodies. They may kiss from time to time. At this stage in the courtship the lovers are too impatient for foreplay, and so they indulge in afterplay instead. Then they get up from the ground and introduce themselves to each other.

This ritual is called "making kikipoopoo." When the young man has made kikipoopoo with a girl five times, the tribe expects that he will marry her.

After marriage the couple put away kikipoopoo with other childish things. When sexually aroused in the marital state, they begin by introducing themselves to each other, proceed to murmured endearments and body caresses, and only then go on to some variety of intercourse.

The tribe, however, has a social problem that for years has been corrupting the structure of this previbrate social order. Since making kikipoopoo five times with the same girl signifies intent to marry, many Orunami boys make kikipoopoo four times and then start on another girl. One Orunami elder has kikipoopooed every woman in the village four times, much to the detriment of Orunami marriage.

On islands lying off Papua and Mamua we find tribes of previbrates whose language is so rich it contains many words to describe the personality of the penis. A "donguta," for example, is a withdrawn and brooding penis. "Shabubba" means "outgoing penis." A "wakipoga" signifies an unpredictable penis. The word "dongudongu" means a reliable penis, and it is the hope of every maiden on the islands to find herself a man with a dongudongu.

These previbrates make much of the deflowering of a virgin. This is a social occasion that the entire tribe attends. It takes place in the Unstable Hut, next to the Long House. Old women of the tribe garland the hut with hibiscus and other spectacular flora. Other women prepare a feast to celebrate the rites. The village elder leads the boy and the virgin girl into the Unstable Hut. The girl lies down on a bed of flower petals, and as the boy begins to deflower her, all the villagers lift their voices in a cheer:

Rah-Rah-Rah!
Sis-boom-bah!
Rutututi,
Futututi,
Poi, poi, yam,
Bam, bam, bam,
Bilabongy,
Basarongi,
Rah-Rah-Rah!
Sis-boom-bah!

At the end of the cheer they shout the names of the girl and the boy. After the girl is deflowered, the young couple shake hands and have a little something to eat.

In these islands the husband follows a quaint ritual

every month at the onset of the wife's menses. When this occurs, he takes the wife back to her parents or next of kin, and asks for a refund on the bride price he has paid. The parents or next of kin then make a ritual refusal. They hop three times on the left foot, three times on the right, and then spit in the husband's eye. The husband then takes the bride back to his hut, where he gives her the "ritetoa oka," or "silent treatment," for three days.

In a corner of Mozambique dwells a tribe that permits weddings only when the moon is full. Before the wedding, the tribe strips the bride and smears her with cymbidium honey from the nose down to the instep. (Cymbidia grow wild and profusely on this island.) Then the entire tribe laps the honey off the girl, to the delight of the groom, who is tied to a tree. Only after they have lapped her clean do they release the groom and allow him to deflower her in the moonlight while the island "wan-itu," or glee club, sings background music *a capella*. From this custom has come our term "honeymoon."

The literature dealing with sexual anthropology is rich and diverse, and we can cover little more here. Those wishing to explore further into those aspects of the past that have created our sexual present will find such study an endless source of personal erotic enrichment. Meanwhile, you might prepare yourself for such studies by kiki-pooing the girl next door.

X
Masturbation for
Middle America

What is masturbation?

Masturbation is the term we apply to any method of achieving orgasm provided you do it all by yourself. In other words, do-it-yourself intercourse. If someone else does it for you we must subsume it under the heading of foreplay.

Many killjoys have written of the evil effects of masturbation: insanity, loss of will power, return of baby fat, exhaustion, ingrown toenails, tennis elbow, and unclean thoughts. All of this, of course, is utter nonsense. While it is true that masturbation loosens the teeth, it is harmless for denture wearers.

If we took the sum total of all the people in this country who swim, play tennis, golf, bridge, and football, drive cars, and vote, the number would represent only one-third of those who masturbate regularly or on a part-time basis. Statistics show that 19,256,187 Americans are masturbating at any given moment of the day. Close your eyes and try to imagine what is going on. Are you overwhelmed? You should not be.

Masturbation has its drawbacks and we must not be blind to them. Perhaps the greatest argument against masturbation is that it is not a good way to meet people, and if you are by nature a loner, it will tend to exacerbate that aspect of your character. Yussuf ibn Farad did not condemn masturbation, although he did say, "I have nothing against the practice but I do hate to grunt in private."

Since masturbation is a solitary occupation, it deprives the masturbator of a companion with whom to hold long pointless discussions about the nature and extent of the orgasm. To overcome this problem, some masturbators talk to themselves after the act, murmuring, "Was it good for you, darling?" and replying in a different voice, "Yes, dear, simply marvelous." Or Voice One asks, "Do you like my right hand better than my left hand?" to which Voice Two replies, "I can't choose between them. Each has something special and different and wonderful to offer. I love them both and I love you, too."

While masturbation is still illegal in some states, the more permissive sexual atmosphere that now exists gives us hope that legislators will strike such laws from the books as soon as they stop jerking off.

The advantages of masturbation are manifold:

1. You don't have to satisfy anyone but yourself.
2. You don't have to rent a motel room.
3. You don't have to talk to yourself afterward unless you feel like it.
4. You don't have to get undressed.
5. You don't have to bathe.
6. You can go right to sleep afterward.
7. You don't have to send yourself flowers.
8. You don't have to use a contraceptive.
9. No one will ask if you want to set up housekeeping.
10. You can treat yourself as a sexual object.
11. You can read a book, watch television, or talk to your lover on the phone at the same time.

With all the advantages that masturbation offers, why should any healthy person hesitate to give himself this pleasure? Mainly because of the psychological remnants of an upbringing that reflected the dying mores of the Victorian era. Yet if we look into history, we must ask ourselves why Buckingham Palace ordered more fat candles during Victoria's reign than under any other regime in British history. And the records show that until death struck him down before his time, Prince Albert always kept both hands in his pants pocket whenever he went strolling in the gardens. We can assume that he kept his Teutonic digits mighty busy diddling his old knockwurst.

Most of us learn to masturbate very early. Girls learn a little more slowly than boys, and usually at a later age, but most of them make up for lost time. Some even stumble upon the secrets of masturbation quite by accident. One young woman never did get the hang of the thing until her house caught fire and a friendly fireman hosed down her clitoris. Unfortunately, this baroque experience turned her to arson.

Physiology limits men in the equipment they can use as aids in masturbation. First we have that old standby the hand, a simple and effective device that hangs from the end of the wrist. By extending the hand, wrapping it around the penis, then raising it and lowering it much in the manner one churns butter, the man can masturbate satisfactorily. Most men prefer to masturbate rather than churn butter even though the manufacture of butter can bring in a tidy income.

Literal-minded men can purchase artificial vaginas. Men who use them most often fill them with air although, as we have suggested previously, it is best to fill them with some nutritious substance. Recommended temperature for the American artificial vagina is 95° Fahrenheit. (European vaginas are centigrade. They come mostly from Switzerland, where Swiss craftsmen size them differently from

their American counterparts. For instance, the Swiss vagina 14BB corresponds to the American vagina 12AAAAA.) When your artificial vagina is not in use, you can fill it with water and put it into the freezer. Later you can pop it into the picnic basket to keep the beer cold.

More imaginative men will follow the lead of Philip Roth and realize that they can put to the service of masturbation almost any yielding substance that is not abrasive. Roth chose liver because it is both yielding and smooth, but we have found it inferior to chopped meat (⅓ pound chuck, ⅓ pound round, ⅓ pound veal, and add a touch of oregano for piquancy). Buy your chopped meat from a reputable butcher and have it ground to order. Prepackaged meats may be cheaper, but whatever you save in pennies you will pay out in ecstasy.

If, like many men, you use smoked whitefish, we say well and good. But watch out for the bones!

For women masturbation indeed offers a brave new world. The hand is but the humblest of the objects that can bring her the joy she seeks, and if she is a daughter of the times she is soon beyond employing the once novel but now passé electric toothbrush. Tumbling from love's cornucopia come the Italian or Hebrew National salami, the zucchini, the well-directed shower-head, the vacuum-cleaner hose, the automobile muffler, the Bonwit Teller mailing piece, the conductor's baton. Again, the uncreative woman will content herself with the artificial penis, although it cannot cool beer efficiently. Like the artificial vaginas, artificial penises come in many varieties, and it is common for famous sports figures and motion-picture actors to model for them. At this writing the most popular artificial penis is the Hank Hansen, named for the Pittsburgh Steelers' outstanding quarterback. (In a contract battle Hansen successfully blocked the Steelers' management from cutting themselves in on the income from his penis.) The Mike Mallory penis was popular for a long time, until a sportswriter exposed it for the forgery it was. Despite the attractive packaging in which the makers present the artificial penis, its appeal is still to the woman who lacks imagination.

Every morning after breakfast make up your schedule for the day. Look at your calendar and find out when you can squeeze in a little masturbation. Perhaps right after the salesmen's meeting and before you have to confer with the company controller. Perhaps you can excuse yourself for a few minutes before you drink your dinner coffee. And certainly at night, when you take off your clothes and your genitalia are so conveniently at hand, you might as well masturbate before putting on your pajamas.

Masturbation has helped many women take the monotony out of household and social chores. When they do the dishes, for instance, they do not simply wash and dry. Instead they wash, masturbate, and *then* dry. And you can see your reflection in those dishes! Others turn their visits to their in-laws into jolly escapades rather than drab obligations by wearing a cordless vibrator when they leave home.

We are just beginning to assess the advantages that a masturbatory work force brings to industry and commerce. Those offices and factories that now allow morning and afternoon masturbation breaks have noted a decrease in absenteeism and an increase in productivity. A similar plan may be in the offing for the United States Congress.

Organize your life so that you have ample time for masturbation. You can adjust any occasion, rearrange any calendar, to accommodate this activity. And remember that especially good times to masturbate are during I.R.S. audits and wedding anniversaries.

XI
You and Your
Loudmouth Body

In recent years science has made an important new discovery: your body talks. Not just your tongue and your larynx, but your entire soma communicates in ways unknown even to yourself. When you learn to read the body language of others you will be well on your way to becoming a better lover, and randy people will go to great extremes to cut you from the herd.

The next time you attend a social gathering where men and women meet and mingle, look around you and notice how so many of the guests say one thing with their mouths while their bodies are saying something very different.

We begin with the most rudimentary example of the way the body talks. A woman may be praising your lean and compact buttocks to the skies, but if she sits down and crosses her legs as she speaks, she is telling you that you will find it rather difficult to make successful sexual advances. (If she crosses her legs very slowly, she is saying the same thing in a stutter.) If she accompanies the crossed legs with a thin-lipped grimace, then rather ostentatiously folds her arms over her breasts and leans forward until her forehead is touching her knees, she is reinforcing this first impression. If, in addition to all this, she lifts her head from her knees just long enough to look at you and make retching sounds, you have every right to conclude that you do not arouse her sexually. If she should then get up and cross *your* legs, then you must definitely turn your attention elsewhere.

But where? Again the language of the body will give you your clue. Look first for a young woman who is sitting or standing with her legs wide apart in the position that scientists call the "Venus straddle." Having found such a woman, try to catch her attention by some gentle stratagem. You might, for instance, sing the first eight bars of "Pale Hands I Loved Beside the Shalimar." As you sing she will probably look at you, and when she does, examine the corners of her mouth for any slight sign that she may be drooling. Next, see if she exhibits signs of body warmth. Is she mopping her brow? Is she unbuttoning the first three buttons of her blouse, pulling the top of her brassiere outward, and blowing down her cleavage? Her body having spoken to you in such friendly terms, you may now feel free to approach her verbally. While it would be considered rather vulgar to give her the "feel direct," it is permissible to ask, "Is Madame moist?" If the answer is in the affirmative you have every right to consider that the young woman is not averse to initiating sexual relations, probably starting with *The Persian Love Apple,* the favored position among new lovers.

Men have their own way of letting their bodies say things that would be improper in verbal communication. If you are a young woman at this social gathering, and you have been celibate for two days and are therefore understandably ferocious, look around the room. When you learn to read body language you will know which man offers the greatest promise of heavenly sexual fulfillment.

Take the young fellow in the corner. He is sitting with his legs crossed, a glass of carrot juice in his left hand, his nose running profusely, his left index finger reaming wax out of one ear, and his other hand riffling through the crematoria section of the Yellow Pages of the phone book. What the man's body is saying in effect is, "My legs are crossed so that you cannot clutch and claw at my penis or heft my scrotum, I am drinking carrot juice so that I can see you at night if you try to break into my room, my nose is running to puncture any dreams you may have about possible cunnilingus, I am cleaning my ear so that I can hear you in case you try tiptoeing into my life, and if you come any closer I am going to kill you and burn the body." Such a man does not make a good prospect.

But what of that fellow standing near the window, one broad shoulder against the wall? In his left hand he holds a martini. His eyes are half closed, but the pupils are dilated and his glance is piercing as he turns from one woman to another, looking each of them straight in the boobs. His breathing is heavy but steady, a few drops of perspiration glisten on his upper lip and you notice with a thrill of anticipation that he sweats in French, his legs are wide apart, and he has an erection. You can be forgiven if you interpret this man's body language to say, "I am interested in a sexual encounter."

Your body will respond to him by making some subtle gesture. Perhaps your left breast will pop out of your dress and wink at him. (For breast-winking cf. the chapter on Sexercises.)

Once you have his attention, it is your body's turn to reply more fully to the message his body has sent you. Without using the medium of speech, you can answer in any number of ways that will be intelligible to him. You might sink slowly to the floor, lie on your back, and extend your legs into the air. This may confuse him at first but sooner or later he will interpret your message in the spirit in which you sent it, and you are ready to begin a meaningful relationship that will add zest to the party.

You have many other body signals that will get across the message that you are interested in some venereal hanky-panky. Let us say you are a woman flying to Salt Lake City, where you plan to try on a Mormon. Next to you sits a man whose general appearance excites you. Put down your magazine, turn your head slightly, let your eyelids half-close, and stare at his crotch without blinking. The chances are excellent that you will elicit some response. When he reacts to your glance by making a gesture in your direction, you might say, "Pardon me, sir, but is that a towel you have stuffed in your crotch?" If he is a gentleman he will deny it, perhaps heatedly. As soon as he calms down you can order a blanket from the stewardess and—voilà! You are well on your way to a new relationship!

A word of warning. It would be feckless for a woman to have too much faith in a bulging crotch no matter how much the man might protest his natural endowment. In all too many cases it is not a true bulge but what the French call *le bombement de ballet,* or the "ballet bulge" so beloved of male dancers. Women have no foolproof method that will guarantee them against being taken in by the false lure of *le bombement de ballet.* In the last analysis, the proof of the pudding is in the eating.

The aggressive man or woman has, albeit unconsciously, a full vocabulary of body movement which the skilled can translate in terms of sexual desire. Smoldering eyes can say more than sonnets. One lover we know is so skilled at smoldering that he can make his irises smoke, either singly or in concert. Moist lips and panting with the tongue out are other signs the prospective lover should seek. Our records also tell of a woman who has developed a highly sophisticated and elegant set of body signals. She may, among other things, sit on the lap of a male guest at a party, and squirm to climax.

Zippers, of course, have a language all their own, and what they say on the way down is nothing at all like what they say on the way up.

Don't be afraid to let your body speak for you!

XII

Everything You Weren't Afraid to Ask about Sex

Thousands of men and women from all over the world have written to Martin Hancock, Recording Secretary of the International Sex Conference, to seek answers to questions about their sexual lives. Here we present the questions most commonly asked, together with the answers the Answer Committee of the Sex Conference provided:

I am seventeen years old and I have been having s-x with my brother since I was fifteen. Is this wrong?

We can see that you were a late starter. No, having s-x with your brother is not wrong unless you fail to take your parents into your confidence. Keeping secrets from your parents is exactly the wrong way to go about building lasting relationships. Don't spoil a good thing!

How big around is the normal penis?

The circumference of the penis depends on seasonal and geographic factors. It varies from an average of two and three-quarter inches during the winter, to three and a half inches in the summer. North of the Arctic Circle the penis has no circumference to speak of. Since the vaginal opening shows the same seasonal and geographic variation, it all comes out even.

We have been unable to get accurate measurements in the Horse Latitudes, where the penis always droops.

Does the size of the penis make any difference in intercourse?

All reputable sex authorities agree that the size of the penis makes absolutely no difference in intercourse. They insist that size does not affect the pleasure potential of either the male or the female in the sex act. And if you can believe that, you can believe anything!

Can I get pregnant from toilet seats?
Not if you sit on them alone.

Is it dangerous to have intercourse with a woman during her menstrual period?

Extremely so. During menses the vagina is usually snappish, ill-tempered, and difficult to control. Remember the old adage: fools rush in.

Does the rhythm system of birth control work?
Only among blacks.

What is the Volvo?

Volvo is nothing more or less than the Swedish spelling of vulva. The Swedes always capitalize it as a mark of respect.

Are two breasts sufficient for a woman?

No. After all, a woman might have triplets or even quintuplets, and you can't keep infants quiet on a chow line. We are not certain where the process of evolution went awry, but we do know that in the space between the two breasts women now sport and the mons veneris there is ample room for four more breasts, two on each side. Even from the survival point of view this would be a much better physiological arrangement, since it would give the dangerously exposed navel much better protection from the elements and from marauding animals.

What is testosterone?

Not *what,* but *who.* Luigi Testosterone (1894-1959) was a famous Italian strong man who appeared for seventeen years with the Ringling Brothers Barnum & Bailey Circus. He was a passionate man by nature, but his career came to an untimely end when he bit off his wife's head during orgasm and thereafter fell out of favor with the authorities.

How many orgasms can a woman have at one session?

This varies in every woman. It depends on how long she can go without food and water. If, however, she stops for a nutritious snack, she will be able to maintain serial orgasms until senility. Once senility sets in, she will have memory trouble and forget to climax.

When I meet a woman, how can I tell if she is interested in having sex with me?

When you first meet a woman, offer to shake her hand. If during the process of shaking your hand she scratches your palm, that means she is interested in having sex with you. If she does not scratch your palm, shake hands with her four or five times during the course of the evening. She may come around.

What is the cervix?

The Cervix is a small four-cylinder foreign car with disc brakes, rack-and-pinion steering, and front-end transmission. An eight-cylinder Cervix is also available, but it is a custom-built car and priced far beyond the reach of the average citizen.

Is frigidity common among women?

Frigidity among women is more than common. It exists in epidemic proportions. It is easy to spot a frigid woman because she tends to have a one-word vocabulary. The word is "no." Whenever you hear that word from the lips of a woman, you are face to face with someone who suffers from frigidity. Such women deserve not opprobrium but sympathy.

I have always heard that men can have only a certain number of ejaculations in the course of a lifetime. To date, I have had 21,634 ejaculations. Am I in trouble?

Brother, are you ever! You have only sixteen orgasms to go. Make them real dandies, and best of luck, old man!

What function do the male nipples serve?

The male nipples are guideposts to help women reach the male navel. If they draw a line from one nipple to the other across the chest, and then extend a line downward from each nipple at an angle of 45°, the lines will cross at the center of the navel.

Do you believe that one-night stands are harmful?

One-night stands represent one of the most beautiful and satisfying relationships between the sexes. Tristan and Isolde, Orpheus and Eurydice, Romeo and Juliet all tried to extend the one-night stand to unmanageable proportions, with dire results to all concerned.

What is the angle of the penis to the vertical during erection?

According to Albert Einstein (1879-1955), the angle is 31°. This figure, however, is sharply at odds with the one arrived at by Enrico Fermi.

Every day I wait at the entrance to the gym in the John Adams High School, and show my penis to the girls as they come out. To date, I have gotten no reaction. What am I doing wrong?

We would have to know exactly how you are showing your penis before we can answer your question. Are you flaunting it in a smart-alecky way? Are you waving it frenetically? Or do you open your raincoat modestly and display your penis without too much fanfare and with a

decent sense of modesty? If the latter is the case and you are still getting no response, perhaps you should try another high school.

Whenever I see a Greyhound bus with a flat left-rear tire, I get very excited sexually. Am I queer?

No, you are not queer. But you are a little unusual.

I have often heard reference to the Aquascutum. Can you tell me what this is?

The Aquascutum is the male contraceptive of choice among the upper classes in Britain.

My girlfriend has erected a small grandstand in her bedroom. It accommodates twenty people. Whenever we have sex, she sells tickets at ten dollars apiece to people who want to watch. The stands are always full and some nights we have to hang out the S.R.O. sign. My question is this: must she declare this money on her income-tax return?

No. Your sexual relations with your girl constitute a nonprofit activity. If, however, your girlfriend charges you as well as the other guests, then she must make full financial disclosure and pay tax accordingly.

Must I ask a woman's permission before toying with her clitoris? I am very confused. Some of my friends say yes but others believe that asking permission is quite unnecessary. I want to do the right thing.

In the early stages of a relationship, before the sex partners know each other very well, most women expect you to ask permission in the interest of good form. You should couch the question politely. "Mizzz Hogan, may I toy with your clitoris?" is a good way to phrase it.

Later, when you and Mizzz Hogan are on a first-name basis, she will acknowledge that an unspoken agreement allows you to toy away without prior verbal sanction.

XIII

The Peripatetic Penis and the Nomadic Clitoris

Why does lovemaking with the same partner tend to lose its edge over the years? What has happened to the breathless anticipation of the courtship days, when every slight touch developed into a grope? What has stood alchemy on its head and turned your eighteen-carat ecstasies into the fool's gold of wham-bam-thank-you-Ma'am? What has muted the orgasmic cry so that it is now little more than a whimper?

In most cases we will find the answer in the word "variety." The average sexual partners settle into a routine, and once fornication becomes routine it becomes dull. The man and woman settle into a rut, and everyone knows that a rut is no place to make love. The partners give forth the same love signals, assume the same position, have sex in the same bed at the same hour and even the same day of the week. Gone is the spontaneity of the early days, when the eager gallant seized his lady fair on impulse and tore off a quick *Crème à la Mignonette* in the broom closet while the maid was vacuuming the living-room rug. Now even love-play follows a set schedule as formal as a minuet. The man and woman lie prone on the bed. Much like the bull in the bullring, the man has his "querencia."

He likes to lie on the left side of the woman and start foreplay by stroking her fifth cervical vertebra just as he always has over the past years.

Sophisticated lovers are aware of the deadening effect of routine. Instinctively, they vary every aspect of lovemaking from day to day. They look upon the bed as only a small part of the ambience of passion, and they are always ready to ride the transports of love in a new locale, thus ensuring the element of surprise and the excitement that new surroundings bring.

Intelligent lovers never shackle lovemaking to a particular hour of the day or night. Each day has twenty-four hours and of these twenty-four each is as good as the next for sexual expression. What is good enough for P.M. is certainly good enough for A.M.

Begin thinking in terms of your house or apartment and then expand your horizons to include the outdoors, indeed the whole great globe itself and the skies above!

You can live your love life in many places other than your bedroom. Why should not a young man thrill his beloved by stretching her out on the ironing board for a fast *gamahuche* and then a leisurely *croupade, chevalade,* or even a simple *Tutti-Frutti.* It will make a welcome change from the too familiar tactile sensations the bed and mattress offer. If the legs of the ironing board are wobbly, ask the children to hold them until you are finished.

You can also make love in all the chairs and on all the tables. If you are imaginative and not hypercritical by nature, you may try one of your bookshelves, where you will find ample maneuvering room for the basic *Upsy-Daisy.*

You do not even need space to lie down in. You can utilize every square foot of your domicile by making love standing up in any of the seventeen Indian positions well known to all of you. Be moderate, however, in your use of Number Nine, the *Punjab Twist,* because too frequent

repetition of this position tends to rupture spinal discs, dislocate the pelvic bone, and distend the bladder. It also lacerates the woman's navel. Yet the *Punjab Twist* is delightful as a once-in-a-blue-moon surprise party.

Lovers who have never made love in a bathtub do not deserve inside plumbing. The temperature of the water should be just right—not hot enough to debilitate the lovers, not cold enough to diminish ardor. Climb into the tub together, holding hands. The woman should lie with her feet spread wide and the man should sit between her feet, his back to the woman's face. Then she can begin love-play by squeezing the blackheads on his back, an enterprise dear to most female hearts. With this done, he might turn and look for nits in her hair. Perhaps she rewards him with a light nibble-kiss for each nit. From this point on be fancy-free and frolic as you will in the intimate tides. Blow bubbles, splash about, sing sea chanties, and pipe Cupid aboard.

As the man in the tub pursues foreplay to its natural conclusion and he is ready to make his entry, he must, if he intends to use the Missionary Position as an exotic change in pace, be very careful in handling his mate. A shocking number of men have drowned their women in this fashion.

Once out of the tub, the lovers can dry each other off with swansdown and then finish the session with a mutual Sloan's Liniment rubdown.

Many lovers who use the tub prefer to fill it with liquids other than water. Champagne and sweet cream head the list, but onion soup, topped off with a slice of toasted French bread and grated cheese, adds an exotic fillip that will delight even the most jaded lover. Small women can use the slice of toast as a raft.

If you are a white-collar worker or professional you will probably find it difficult to copulate during office hours, but difficult is not the same thing as impossible. Surely you can manage a little sex between business appointments, unless it interferes with your masturbation schedule. And even if you can't, your fellow workers are surely sensitive enough to look the other way if you boff your secretary between invoices. Or she may conceal herself beneath your desk during a staff meeting and, unbeknownst to others, oblige you with a daring act of fellatio to express her loyalty to the firm. In return, you may ask her to stay after hours, when the reception room is empty and you can delight her with a *Frank-on-a-Roll*. She will be doubly pleased because she will be drawing overtime pay. All the world loves a lover, so do not worry about the charwoman. She will be considerate enough to mop around you.

Construction workers on skyscrapers have a different problem. It takes very long to get down from the steel beams and just as long to get back up. Perhaps when more women work in the industry they will help men learn how to perform some elementary positions on the girders. Meanwhile, the best thing for construction workers to do is quit. Construction work is quite dangerous anyway.

Sandhogs face analogous difficulties, yet this is not too important since our surveys reveal sex to be primarily a middle- and upper-class preoccupation. The lower classes tend to bowl rather than copulate.

A wonderful way to bring exciting variety to the sex act is to leave your house behind you and "vacation" for an afternoon or an evening in a motel. You can register under an assumed name, and this alone is a ploy that has brought many a young woman to a delicious orgasm. New surroundings, the mechanical Hepplewhite bed that jiggles up and down when you put a quarter in the slot, and the dirty movies on the tube will heighten every aspect of your lovemaking. And if you are lucky you might hear the young woman in the next room gasp the Gettysburg Address through the papier-mâché walls.

You will return to your real home renewed in spirit, relaxed and languid in body, and ready for your next adventure: making love on a high wire stretched over Niagara Falls.

The great outdoors, the fields and meadows, the streets, the public parks and children's playgrounds, all beckon lovers to foreplay and fulfillment. Who can forget Mudflat Higgins, second baseman for the Mets, who, during the seventh-inning stretch in a crucial game with Philadelphia, led his lady fair onto the field, tucked second base beneath her buttocks, and put the boots to her then and there to the acclamation of the enthusiastic crowd? And when her orgasmic cries went out over the P.A. system, Kate Smith sang "God Bless America" and the fans rose to their feet to pay tribute to Mudflat and his adorable Joan Quigley Hargrove. For this Mudflat won the Heisman Trophy that year, even though the award committee usually reserves that honor for football players. (In the same year a quarterback for the Miami Dolphins won the Cy Young Award for buggering a Cotswold ewe during a huddle on his own forty-eight-yard line.)

Love amid the beauties of nature is especially rewarding. Lovers who entwine their limbs in dells and dales, 'mid bowers and arbors, find they draw power and energy from these primeval surroundings. True, lovers sometimes suffer untoward effects from outdoor escapades. The backward fuzz bust some of them and drag them off, kicking and screaming, to the paddy wagon. Others draw spectators who may heckle or comment on faulty technique, and one young woman later suffered from a vaginal infestation of chipmunks. But risks such as these are slight when compared to the delights all lovers experience in the field, where they literally expand their sexual horizons.

Next time you take a commercial flight, try making love in the plane's galley with the curtains drawn. It is best to do this after the stewardesses have served the meal and are sitting aft, dreaming of Mr. Right. If you make love in a light single-engine, four-seater plane, be careful not to distract the pilot.

One man we know claims that his most tantalizingly beautiful sexual experience came when he assaulted his beloved in a canoe on the Central Park lake, using the Missionary Position. As a result, she has ruts in her back from the cross-ribs. Even though he must now wear snow tires when he enters her from the rear, he considers the sacrifice well worth it.

Another enticing spot that beckons the adventurous lovers is the rest room of your local Exxon station. If you use these facilities, be sure to report to the manager any signs of untidiness. He will take corrective action at once.

Sit down right away and make out an itinerary for the peripatetic penis and the nomadic clitoris. Select the unusual places that attract you both, and the bliss you were once afraid of losing will fill all your future venereal encounters.

XIV
Releasing the Horny Child
Inside All of Us

Do you have in the back of your mind a number of cute little sex games you would like to play but are too embarrassed to suggest to your partner? Chances are your partner feels exactly as you do. After all, copulation isn't *all* work, and fun and games are an important part of every experience, with the possible exception of major surgery and death. Sharing secret sex romps brings lovers closer together.

At times passion overrides all else and the sexual encounter reaches such a peak that it engulfs body, mind, and soul. At other times, however, sex is a frolic, a hop, skip, and a jump, and you are missing a great deal if you do not approach it in that spirit. Open Venus's hope chest and take out the childlike but sweet little games you have always wanted to play. The next time you are ready for sex, be it in bed or on a 747, suggest them to your partner. If he or she faints, suggest something else.

You may begin with this common game, which becomes great fun when played as a prelude to full penetration. The woman seats herself nude on the carpet, linoleum, or flagstones of the patio, knees bent, legs spread wide. The man sits in a similar position facing her. He puts his feet across her feet and pushes his pelvis forward until his penis rests lightly but firmly on her labia. Then he deals a hand of casino. Instead of points, each player wins a position. If the woman holds the Big Casino she wins one *Willy's Wheelbarrow*. The Small Casino is worth one *St. Catherine's Wheel*. The player who amasses the most positions gets a free bonus of a *Chevalade à la Napoleon*. Sex casino almost always induces gay laughter and an elfin spirit, and it is a game in which even the loser wins.

We all love theatricals, and no time is more fitting for psychodrama than during foreplay. Act out your fantasies. Whom do you want to come to bed as next? Herbert Hoover? Zorro? Or would you like to wear a monkey suit? Any of these alter egos is entirely appropriate. Let us say that you are Sherlock Holmes. You work out a little drama with the cooperation of your sweet little friend. Her clitoris has committed murder most foul and you must find clues that lead to the killer. Make that search thorough and painstaking. Is that a hair under her armpit or a blade of grass from the highlands north of Glasgow? Does the gravel in her navel come from the driveway of Lord Haversham? Follow each clue until you come face-to-face with the guilty party.

One couple found great pleasure in a charming psychodrama all their own. They loved to play this little game, which they called "Second Story." He would leave the house, put on a stocking mask, tuck a Saturday-night special into his belt, climb the trellis to the balcony outside the bedroom, break through the French windows, throw himself upon the bed, and "rape" his partner. Over the years they developed many spine-tingling variations on this ritual and they enacted it with intense pleasure until the very day the police shot him on the balcony.

Cross-dressing is another form of innocent fun. (We now know that Ben Franklin, in real life a woman, was so popular a figure at the French court because she always cross-dressed.) Cross-dressing gives men and women the opportunity to express their bisexualism and to develop a deeper understanding of each other's underwear.

Many couples find pleasure in looking at or reading pornography. (We define pornography as anything that tends to be dirty in literature or the visual arts.) When looking at pornography together, couples will get the fullest satisfaction only if they join each other in full-throated exclamations such as "Ooh! . . . Aaaah! . . . Look at that one, will you! . . . Whose leg is that anyway? . . . What a great cocksperson!" Shared comments during the perusal of pornography prepare men and women to communicate in all social situations.

In recent years technology has broadened the horizons of sex play with the invention of the tape-recording machine. Nothing brings more satisfaction to a couple than a library of tape-recorded orgasms. You can begin your collection at once and join the growing number of people who take joy in this wholesome hobby. Although tape machines have not been with us very long, historically speaking, hundreds, nay, thousands of extremely valuable collections are already in existence. Pierre Boucher's library of 3,200 Chinese orgasms in Lyons, France, is a treasure house of Oriental concupiscence. And next week the estate of Harlow McKenzie, famed television repairman, will go on the block at the Parke-Bernet Galleries. Included in that estate is the rare and justly famous McKenzie Library of Tapes. Although quantitatively the library is small, consisting of only thirty-two spools, in quality it is unsurpassed. Thirty-one of these tapes represent the only collection extant of the tape-recorded orgasms of members of the D.A.R. The thirty-second records the orgasms of a nymphomaniacal hippopotamus.

The McKenzie estate expects to realize more than a

million dollars from its sale. Let us hope that the collection does not go to Kuwait. It is a national treasure and it belongs in the United States.

Couples who are not interested in collecting should at the very least keep a library of their own tape-recorded orgasms. It is always pleasant to listen to them on a snowy night when the logs are crackling in the fireplace and the dog is in the woods, violating opossums. You can have friends in and take much mutual joy in comparing sounds. You can index your private collection either by date or by decibel level. Perhaps the latter is the best system, because you can easily find the quiet or the noisy orgasm that best fits your mood when you sit down to listen.

And when you and your beloved are old and gray, you can always snuggle up, hold hands, and listen to the orgasms of your youth.

XV
Beat Me, Daddy,
Eight to the Bar

We derive the word "sadism" from the Marquis de Sade (1740-1814), founder of the French Cub Scouts and organizer of the first ground-glass cookie sale. A sadist is one who finds gratification in inflicting pain on another person or surrogate person, such as a pussycat.

For the word "masochism" we are indebted to the Austrian novelist Leopold von Sacher-Masoch. A masochist is anyone who likes sadists. Leopold von Sacher-Masoch was a curious chap who used to strip nude, have a friend paint the word "welcome" on his back, and then lie face-down in front of the door to his house. Any visitor who wiped his feet could bring Sacher-Masoch to climax.

Infinite are the varieties of love, and nothing better expresses this infinitude than the urge, common to about 20 percent of all lovers, to beat or be beaten as a form of foreplay. This is known as sadomasochism, or S.M. for short.

Lest you think that S.M. is a rare deviation, consider the words of Holzen-Verdücke, who wrote, "In my laboratory I conducted twelve experiments to see if I could swing a cat without hitting a sadomasochist. I failed. As I swung the cat for the thirteenth time, I ejaculated. It was a beautiful experience." Holzen-Verdücke, by the way, is the only twentieth-century German to boast two umlauts over one "u." The Weimar Republic awarded him the extra umlaut for suffering above and beyond the call of duty.

It is too easy to think of sadomasochism as a way of working out aggressions. The average couple relieve aggressions in a less extreme manner. Four three-minute rounds with twelve-ounce gloves usually dispel hostility between lovers.

The citizenry of civilized countries accept sadomasochism for what it is: a legitimate form of sexual activity in which men and women express their affection for each other in a rather odd but beguiling manner. The commonest form of sadomasochism is bondage. In bondage, one or the other of the sex partners delights in being hog-tied, chained, manacled, or otherwise restrained. Usually it is the man who ties the woman's hands and feet to the bedposts. This places the man in what scientists call the "dominant position," and the woman "behind the eight ball."

If you and your mate want to find tranquillity and inner peace in sadomasochism, you can do so at very little expense. The largest item in your budget will be the indispensable four-poster bed. You can buy your other equipment—tire chains, bullwhips, and the like—for a song ("They're Hanging Danny Deever in the Morning").

In tying your woman to the bedposts, be sure to use knots that you can easily untie in case of fire or other emergency. For tying the hands most lovers prefer the Diamond Knot, which is highly ornamental, although either the Blackwell Hitch or the Englishman's Tie will do nicely. A good round turn and a half hitch over the ankles to the bedposts will adequately secure the feet. In this position a woman can offer only token resistance when you put out your cigarette on her instep. And it is just as well. The serious lover does not smoke during foreplay.

Not all men, however, like to tie their women to the bedposts. Some prefer tying their wrists together and then suspending them from the rafters. This is difficult in modern apartments, where rafters are few and far between, and although some sadomasochistic urbanites install their own, rafter-suspension is prevalent mainly among suburbanites and country folk. Farmers suspend many naked women from the crossbeams in the barn. This is particularly true of dairy farmers. Other men, both urban and rural, take pleasure in breaking their women on the wheel. (Sears, Roebuck offers a good wheel in its sporting-goods section). Broken women, say these men, make the best sex partners. Women, however, have been content not to comment.

It is a common practice among dentists to strap their women patients to the dental chair, and although the profession frowns on the practice, leaders of the American Dental Association usually look the other way.

Women who submit willingly and eagerly to such modes of love are usually the passive type, although now and then one may scream, "Help! Help!" These cries for help are warm and appealing and make for remarkably intense intercourse.

Whipping is another form of foreplay which brings delight to many. All reputable saddle stores offer a wide variety of whips, and if the stock does not appeal to you they will be happy to make one to order. Specify the number of thongs and whether you want them tipped with bauxite fishhooks. Some stores sell His and Hers whips, in an attractive goatskin case. The roll of gauze included in the package is courtesy of the house.

The standard procedure is for the man to lower the

woman's panties, bend her over a chair or a bed, and flay her until her backside turns a rosy red. At the first sign of blood he will, if he is a gentleman, hand her the whip and let her take a turn on him. He will, of course, freely lower his own pants and show good grace as he bends over. During the action both will murmur endearments. When both backsides are streaked with "the rosy fingers of dawn," the lovers will take things to their logical conclusion, perhaps trying the *Hyjerabad Swirl* or a simple *Apple Brown Betty*. Possibly the tenderest part of such an encounter comes in the languid postcoital period, when the lovers gently apply Band-Aids to each other's bottoms, then wash the whips with saddle soap. Nothing is more of a sexual turn-off than a dirty whip.

Whipping has many rituals and often leads to other physical activities. One man we know concludes the whipping ritual by stuffing the breast of his beloved into an Osterizer and turning it on to "blend," but most sadomasochistic circles consider this *de trop*.

Many people try to suppress their natural sadomasochistic feelings, and they do so at the expense of a full and rewarding sex life. Thousands of men have developed ulcers because they have suppressed the desire to give their loved ones the beatings they so intensely crave. One woman wrote us to say, "For twelve years my husband and I had sexual intercourse every Monday, Wednesday, and Friday. I can't begin to tell you how boring it was to look in the mirror and see him thumping away as though thumping were in short supply. We tried everything to bring some excitement and exhilaration into our sex life. He thumped me in the pickup truck, he thumped me in the choir loft, he even thumped me on the McCormick reaper. God, but it was dull, dull, dull! Then one day he came into the house unexpectedly. I happened to be lying

nude on the kitchen table, slapping my genitalia with a flyswatter. My husband roared like a lion, tied me to the table with baling wire, then beat me with a bullwhip until I climaxed. And that is how he saved our marriage."

Love stimulates the sadomasochistic imagination. One couple, always creative in their lovemaking, have transformed their suburban home into a showplace. They fitted the interior like the Tower of London, with racks, wheels, and cauldrons of boiling oil. Since they also use the oil in cooking, it is not an added expense. They have built a deep moat that meanders sweetly around the entire house. An electrically powered drawbridge spans this moat, and in the center of the drawbridge is a trapdoor. Whenever they feel sexually aroused, they call the liquor store, then wait by the window for the delivery boy to appear with his precious wares. Their excitement by this time is intense. When the delivery boy arrives, they lower the drawbridge. Just as the boy reaches the halfway point across the bridge, they spring the trap. The boy falls through the trapdoor into the moat, and drowns. At this stage in the ritual they both reach a beautiful simultaneous climax, during which the woman moans in Elizabethan cadences. They lie down and surrender for a time to the delicious lethargy that usually follows fully satisfying sex. Then they drain the moat and recover the booze. Now that they are fully at ease with themselves and ready for sleep, the man drives a stake into the ground in the backyard. He chains his beloved to the stake for the night. As an earnest of his affection for her, and because the gesture adds a certain *panache* to the evening, he always leaves a bowl of water near her.

Perhaps you are one of millions who daydream about contusions and lacerations and secretly yearn to season your sex with mayhem yet are ashamed to confess to the impulse. If so, you are doing both yourself and your lover a serious disservice. Like olives, excruciating pain is an acquired taste. Look on physical love as a martini. Then ask yourself, "What is the martini without the olive?"

XVI
The Orifice Party

Like most modern lovers you will want to expand your sexual horizons by sharing your love with as many other people as possible. Inevitably, the time will come when you will look upon sexual activity not as a secret matter that you and your sex partner must conduct in selfish privacy behind closed doors but as a social event that you want your friends and loved ones to share to the full. If you are convinced, as are most people in high I.Q. brackets, that ecstasy is worth spreading around, you will want to experience the sharing and the mutual joy that the orgy offers.

When uptight, trashy people use the word "orgy," they give it a pejorative implication, but we will not shy away from its use or try to invent some niggling self-conscious neologism. Think of the orgy as a bacchanalia of togetherness, a breathtaking total experience, an opportunity to see and enjoy all the facets on the diamond of total sex.

The diffident lover who is wary about new experiences and therefore hesitates to take the gang-bang plunge, should proceed slowly. He or she should start with what is known as "threezies," a modest group of three. If the lover is a man, the extra woman he invites should be on friendly terms with his regular female sex partner, or else the girls might exchange words. Strip the two women and yourself. Have them stretch out on a bed large enough to allow you room to kneel between them. Begin with a gentle massage, devoting one hand to each woman. Continue the massage until they both respond with slight undulations of the abdominal region. You may interpret these undulations as a signal to proceed to other acts of foreplay.

Now you must decide whether to go to the breasts or take the gung-ho route of the clitoris. Since you have a sense of the order of things, you decide upon the breasts. Initially it will come as a shock that you have four of these to contend with—an embarrassment of riches. Some threezy men believe in kissing and gently sucking both breasts of one partner and then turning to the other. Others believe in dealing with each breast as an individual. They might, for instance, fondle the left breast of one woman and then the right breast of the other, after which they will take care of those mammaries that have been left out in the cold.

The time has come for you to turn to the clitoris you have so sorely neglected, and you face the problem common to all threezies: you have only one tongue. Clearly, you must titillate one clitoris orally and one manually. This will not be a traumatic situation if you understand your threezy women psychologically. Will one or the other feel that you have relegated her to the status of "second banana" if she has to receive you manually rather than orally? This may not be as insolvable as it sounds if your titillation is furious enough to distract the woman from undue subjectivity. In all fairness, however, after a few minutes of clitoral stimulation you should switch around so that each woman gets the full benefit of your oral and digital ministrations, no one feels slighted, and you get to know both of them better.

So far so good. But the devil has work for idle hands. It is time for intercourse! And now it is not a question of the lady or the tiger, an easy choice. Is it this lady—or that lady? With whom shall you start? The best method, and the one that causes the least ill feeling, is to let the women toss a coin. In the tradition of threezies, the woman on the left tosses and the woman on the right calls the toss. Assume whatever position you and the winner choose, and begin at once. The inactive woman may watch, murmur words of encouragement, or simply relax with a good book until her moment comes. Here the male lover must never, under any circumstances, break a cardinal rule of threezies. He must not remain with the first woman so long that he is unable to penetrate the second woman. Genteel lovers consider this to be in extremely bad taste.

When two men and one woman compose the threezy group, the problems are far less complicated, and after the toss of the coin to determine which man starts first, all the woman has to do is continue until the men are of no use to her anymore. Then she may send out for a second pair of men, or take a glass of milk and a refreshing nap.

After threezies we move on to fourzies as part of our preparation for plenary orgies. Fourzies usually involve two couples who are on good terms with each other and have a very large bed. (Only couples with a strong inclination toward anal penetration would consider fourzies on a single bed.)

Begin fourzies with a mutual massage, using scented massage oils, whipped cream, whipped butter (lightly salted), or Philadelphia cream cheese. After massage, the men and women may investigate whatever proclivities they have toward bisexualism. (Fess up, now! Aren't you bisexual *au fond*? And if not, why not?) Be careful, however,

not to let fourzies degenerate into the standard and rather routine toozies, even if the toozy partners are of the same sex. Mix things up. Be a Leonardo of lubricity. Go from breast to scrotum, from clitoris to penis, from lips to moustache to navel to armpit, and let cries of "Evoe!" ring from your throat. Do not miss any golden opportunity.

The etiquette of fourzies demands that each man have both women at least once, and each woman have both men at least twice. Fourzies can be very confusing. You must always know exactly where you are and what you are doing at any given moment. When finished, be careful in disentangling the various limbs, and do try to remember everyone by name.

Most people go away from their first session of fourzies spiritually refreshed, with a new sense of innocence, and a feeling of meditative calm. Others are exhausted.

Now you are ready for your first orgy. Is there an opening for a new lover in one of your neighborhood orgies? Perhaps not. How, then, do you go about organizing your own orgy? Perhaps the best way to begin is to canvas your own apartment house or, if you are a suburbanite, the houses on your street. Do not expect results without the grass-roots work of ringing doorbells. When someone answers the door, state your case simply and get right to the point. You might begin with a little venial lie. Say that you recently moved to the neighborhood from Phoenix, home of the desert orgy, where you were an Orgy Leader. You are homesick for your old orgy, and you wonder whether it might not be possible for you to organize a new one in the neighborhood. A human approach such as this usually begets a human response.

Once you have interested six or more people (six is the legal quorum for a registered orgy), you can proceed to elect an Orgy Leader. You yourself might be elected because of your experience in Phoenix.

Things may not go smoothly at your very first orgy. There will be little problems to iron out, wheels to be oiled, gears to be shifted before the machinery runs smoothly. Here is an important rule to help speed you on your way: no matter how large your orgy, you must strive for the proper sexual balance, by which we mean you must either have an equal number of each sex, or a modest preponderance of men over women. When the women outnumber the men it always makes some of the men feel inadequate and some of the women extremely testy.

If you are a man and you take your sex partner to her first orgy, she may react in a strange way. Be prepared for tears. A woman often cries at her first orgy. This is natural, and if you give her a tissue and tell her to blow her nose, she will regain her composure and lie down on the piano again.

Let us suppose, as is most likely the case, that a number of established orgies operate in your neighborhood. You can shop around for what suits you best. Ask yourself what kind of orgy fits your personality. First we have the Simple Orgy, a modest affair which provides no services, and to which you must bring your own towels. The Catered Orgy includes a formal supper, a bartender, and waiters. The help will not accept gratuities in the form of money, but if they can expect sexual generosity the service will be excellent. The Buffet Orgy offers a sideboard with cold cuts, one or two hot dishes, and a light wine. This is a self-service orgy. The Al Fresco, or Outdoor, Orgy may be either Simple, Catered, or Buffet, but we will not deal with it here since it is popular only in warmer climates. (The Northeastern states have Al Fresco Orgies but they are strictly seasonal.)

In your eagerness, do not rush to join the first orgy you come across. Remember that you are shopping for something that you will want to last you for a long time,

and you can be very unhappy if you find yourself involved with the wrong one. Let us face it: some orgies do not attract a nice class of people. Look for the significant signs that indicate whether the orgy you plan to join is socially acceptable. If it accepts dogs as members, stay away. Wouldn't it be ironic if, after a sexual encounter, you came down with rabies? And it is quite enough to lie around in a room ringing with orgasms without having to put up with barking, too.

Is the orgy located in a good part of town? Is the atmosphere friendly, or do the participants sock each other with foam-rubber bats to act out their basic antagonisms? Nothing is more repelling than an orgy whose members do not get along with each other. Lastly, find out if one of the orgiasts plays the guitar. First-rate orgies always have at least one fat guitarist to lead in the singing when the breathing returns to normal.

Very well. You have selected your orgy. Do not be precipitate in signing up. Try your orgy a few times. Then and only then, when you are sure you are happy with it, pay your dues and get your locker. Thereafter, whenever you attend your orgy, always make sure you bring your locker key. Although other members of the orgy might try to put a good face on it, they hate sharing their lockers and you may encourage hostility. (This does not apply to those who choose to join one of the increasingly popular Hostile Orgies.) If you have chosen a Simple Orgy with no services, it might be wise to take along a sandwich and a thermos of coffee in addition to the towels.

The etiquette of the orgy is important. Tradition has established a series of rules which you must never violate. Remember that the orgy is not a dance floor and it is very bad form to cut in. If you see someone you would like to use, wait patiently until he or she is finished, offer congratulations, and then express your interest. The experienced orgiast will receive you warmly. Do not hog the best bed or couch. Show yourself to be modest and undemanding by using the clothes closet once or twice. If yours is a Buffet Orgy, never try anything but the Missionary Position on the buffet table, and if you are a man, do keep your woman's backside out of the onion dip.

Some day you will want to achieve the goal of all orgiasts: membership in a Restricted Orgy. Do not let the term "Restricted Orgy" send you running to your nearest Civil Rights Commission. Restricted Orgies are open to people of any race, creed, or color, but these orgies admit only those applicants who score at least seven on the Cockburn Scale, which rates sexual performance on a scale of one to ten. To get your rating, go to any licensed sex critic (you will find one in your sensitivity group), and he will supply you with a surrogate young man or woman to put you through the basics: a Missionary, a *crevissade*, elementary cunnilingus or fellatio, and one *chevalade*. You are bound to be nervous when taking the test, but remember that the sex critic wants you to pass as much as you do.

Although not everyone can join it, the Restricted Orgy is by far the most satisfying. If it is not a goal you can reach at once, membership in such an orgy is something you can and must strive to achieve.

A final word of advice: when leaving your orgy make sure you take the right coat.

XVII
Death of a Hero

Yussuf ibn Farad, pioneer and visionary, never achieved that goal to which he dedicated his entire life: Permanent Orgasm. He was a man too far ahead of his time because the technology that could reify his dream did not yet exist. In this, he was much like Leonardo, who developed a theory of heavier-than-air flight before the discovery of those energy sources that made such flight possible.

After Yussuf and his Shulamite introduced foreplay, in the year 3025 B.C., he wandered throughout the Near and Middle East, patiently teaching, explaining, spreading the joyous word. Disciples of both sexes flocked to his banner, a jaunty affair made of two thousand foreskins lovingly sewn together. How it must have lifted desert hearts to see it fluttering in the *humseen*!

At times the achievement of Permanent Orgasm appeared to be just around the next sand dune, but by the time Yussuf and his disciples returned to normal breathing at the next oasis, the evanescent prize had wafted away like mist beneath the morning sun.

Yussuf never stopped trying until that fatal day in the year 3011 B.C. (?) when he died nobly while performing an extended *Duck-for-the-Lotus-Blossom* on a cooperative Philistine lovely with whom he had an assignation two miles north of Gath. Unfortunately, Yussuf forgot to bring his breathing tube, and he suffocated.

Today Yussuf's body lies mortified in some far and unknown desert, yet the world thinks of his last resting place as a thing of flowers and singing birds, a visionary shrine. Yussuf lives on in the lower abdominal regions of all mankind. On that glorious day when we, his modern disciples, finally achieve Permanent Orgasm, we will have paid our debt to him.

As for Yussuf ibn Farad's gallant Shulamite, we know little other than that shortly after her historic encounter in the sheep meadow, she migrated to Babylon, where she opened the Happy Hour Massage Parlor. Then she drifted into the impenetrable shadows of history.